BREAKING THE NEWS

WHAT'S REAL, WHAT'S NOT, AND WHY THE *difference* MATTERS

ROBIN TERRY BROWN

FOREWORD BY SUSAN GOLDBERG, EDITOR IN CHIEF, NATIONAL GEOGRAPHIC

NATIONAL GEOGRAPHIC
WASHINGTON, D.C.

To Matthew and Cate, may you always follow your curiosity and seek truth.

—ROBIN TERRY BROWN

How to use this book

Breaking the News is packed with information to help you understand the media: the history of news, so you know how it all started; the news today, in its many forms (print, digital, televised, radio, etc.); and how technology may change news in the future. Throughout this book, look for these extra features and boxes of information:

PROFILES
These short biographies highlight people who have made major contributions to journalism or media in general. We couldn't fit every important person, so these are some who have changed the way news is reported.

FAMOUS FLUB
Look for this symbol to spot a "Famous Flub" in news history. Responsible journalists always do their best to get the facts right. But, occasionally, mistakes slip through. This feature shows some of the biggest mistakes the media have ever made.

HEY, THAT'S A HOAX!
Hunt for this symbol to find all of the "Hey, That's a Hoax!" features. We all know that a lot of false news spreads on social media. But false news was around long before the internet. These features show some of the funniest and most interesting hoaxes in history.

POP-UP FACTS
Some pages feature fascinating facts. You can find the sources for all of these facts at the back of the book on page 150.

QUOTES
Many famous people have spoken out about the power and importance of the media. A few of these meaningful quotes are sprinkled throughout the book.

QUESTIONS TO GET YOU THINKING
Keep an eye out for this icon to find questions that encourage you to think about how the information in this book applies to your life. After you read the page, take a moment to pause and consider how you would answer these questions.

A PICTURE IS WORTH A THOUSAND WORDS
This feature appears at the end of chapters 1 through 5 and highlights the importance of photography in telling stories. Short text alongside each image explains what appears in the photo and why it is so important. The camera icon appears next to each of these features.

Media vary a lot from one country to another. All of the information in this book applies to the United States, unless otherwise noted.

Disclaimer
Most social media sites require users to be 13 or older. It's important to follow these rules, as there is a lot of information online that is not appropriate for kids. And be sure to always check with a parent before going online.

CONTENTS

FOREWORD

> ## "If your **mother** says she **loves you,** check it out."

When I was a young reporter in my first job, a veteran newspaperman pulled me aside and gave me this classic bit of journalism advice. (When I told my mother about it, she was not amused. But I got the point: that it's important to verify facts, even those that seem self-evident.)

Although this expression takes professional skepticism to an extreme—of course your mother loves you!—the essence of this advice is more important now than it's ever been.

Today, it can be hard to know what, or whom, to believe. With so much information bombarding us 24/7, on platforms as varied as printed pages, Snapchat, and viral videos, how can we sort out real news from fake? What are the tip-offs that we're reading a fact-based story instead of one that's largely fiction? When we seek information that we can trust, how can we judge what's objective and what's biased?

At *National Geographic*, I like to say that our journalism is on the side of science, on the side of facts, and on the side of the planet. If these principles matter to you, this book can guide you in supporting them, especially the first two. It's a brief course in how to become media literate, at a time when that matters more than ever.

YOU'LL LEARN HOW TO

- Tell if a website is fake;
- Detect phony photos;
- Become an expert fact-checker;
- Use our "Truth Tool Kit" to sniff out fabricated sources;
- Uncover your own biases (we all have them); and
- Become more open-minded about information you might not agree with.

While you're building these media literacy skills, you'll read some fascinating stories about the history of news, as well as how today's journalists work to uncover the facts and share them with global audiences. We'll also do our best to look ahead, to see how future modes of reporting and delivering news could affect us all.

Susan Goldberg, editor in chief
of *National Geographic* magazine

Being media literate is the first step toward becoming an informed consumer, a critical thinker, and an educated guardian of our democracy. Thank you. And if that sounds like a lot to take on, just remember the basics: When your mother says she loves you, check it out!

Susan Goldberg

EDITOR IN CHIEF,
NATIONAL GEOGRAPHIC

EDITORIAL DIRECTOR,
NATIONAL GEOGRAPHIC PARTNERS

INTRODUCTION

It's the blizzard of the century! Snow has been falling for 24 hours and the storm is still going strong. Cars look like giant white marshmallows in people's driveways. The roads have disappeared under a blanket of snow. How much more snow will fall? How long will schools be closed? When will the roads be passable? Is it OK to meet friends for an epic sled-a-thon, or is it so cold and windy that you have to stay inside? How do you find the answers to all these questions?

You flip on the TV and see the weatherperson pointing to maps and making predictions. Then the camera cuts to a reporter standing knee-high in snow to show you just HOW MUCH has accumulated. You grab a phone and tap the weather app, and of course you check out the awesome snowman photos people have posted online. Meanwhile, your mother checks social media to see what people are saying about the road conditions, and your dad fires up the battery-powered radio in case the electricity goes out.

You find information everywhere, and you haven't even left your house. How much of this qualifies as news, and how much is just rumor and chitchat? It is not always easy to tell the difference.

And the avalanche of information doesn't stop when the storm is over. Sports, politics, scandals, celebrities, the latest movies, a five-alarm fire—it just keeps coming. With news, information, and gossip always at your fingertips, how do you know what separates real news from everything else?

WHAT IS NEWS?

Television, radio, the internet, social media, print newspapers and magazines, and some blogs are all sources of news. But no matter where a story appears, journalists and editors must make decisions every day about which events they think qualify as news and which topics are most important. Should the story be the lead for the nightly news? Should it appear at the top of the website or "above the fold" of the newspaper, or should it go on the bottom of page 5 instead?

To decide where the news publishes or if it is even covered at all, news editors consider many questions: Is the story happening now? Is it important and interesting? Is it in the public's interest to report on the story? Is it surprising or unusual?

Audience also plays an important role in an editor's decision. How relevant is the subject to readers of a certain publication or viewers of a particular show? A newspaper in a small farming town might include an article about the sale of a local farm, whereas a New York City paper might feature an article about subway repairs. In the same way, national news outlets in the United States will focus on topics that most interest their American audience, and a paper from India might focus on events in its capital, New Delhi.

Every day's news is different, but the questions that editors ask stay very much the same.

IS IT POSSIBLE TO BE Objective?

People often say that a journalist's job is to be objective—which means they don't let their personal feelings or beliefs affect how they deliver the news. Today, journalists understand that it's impossible for any human being to be 100 percent objective. The town and country people live in, the culture they grew up in, and even the languages they speak will influence what they think is important and interesting. Journalists are no different. Their backgrounds impact the stories they choose to cover and how they cover them.

Responsible journalists focus on being aware of their opinions and beliefs, or biases, and try to keep them in check. How? By reporting only the facts and information they can verify with reliable sources. They also share these sources in their stories. So if readers have questions about the news as it's presented, they have enough information to dig deeper on their own.

Crowds capture a ceremony in Beijing, China, on their smartphones. It can be hard to tell the difference between images like these, posted online, and the news.

Where Do **Kids & Teens** (ages 10 to 18) *Get Their News?*

63%
FAMILY, TEACHERS & FRIENDS

49%
SOCIAL MEDIA & THE INTERNET

46%
TV, PRINT NEWSPAPERS & RADIO

*Survey participants could select more than one answer.

HOW JOURNALISTS DO THEIR JOBS

Today, just about anyone can post information, opinions, and photos on a website or social media. So what's the difference between all of this chatter and true news? It comes down to the purpose of journalism—to provide information that is accurate, fair, and balanced so people can make smart decisions about their families, communities, and governments. Unlike people who are not trained journalists, reporters have an organized system for gathering information and verifying facts to ensure that stories are true.

Journalists rely on a combination of interviews, research, and firsthand accounts from people who were present when important events took place. During a snowstorm, for example, a journalist may turn to the National Weather Service to find out about snowfall predictions; to local police and firefighters to find out about weather-related emergencies; to school officials to find out about school closures; and to regular people to find out how the storm is affecting their day-to-day lives. That's a lot different from someone on social media saying they "heard" schools were closing or your dad saying, "Yup, looks like there's at least 10 feet of snow outside."

Journalists often get information from local and national governments, hospitals, and courthouses, as well as from scientists, experts, witnesses, and others. They try to go straight to the original source of a story and then they follow the "two-source rule," meaning that they confirm stories with two people who have direct knowledge of the topic.

This method of gathering and fact-checking information separates news from all other information. The true purpose of these stories is to provide information that is in the public interest. Most important, journalists do their best to get a story right. And when they get it wrong, they immediately publish a correction.

KNOW YOUR NEWS

Today, the role of trained journalists is more important than ever. With social media and the internet quickly becoming leading sources of news and information, it's harder to tell where information is coming from and if it's accurate. This book will give you the tools to understand the news, so you can decide what to believe.

A Washington, D.C., reporter interviews children sledding near the U.S. Capitol building during a March 2015 snowstorm.

TYPES OF News

Press conferences, like this one given by German chancellor Angela Merkel at the 2019 European Union Summit, can be a source of breaking news.

Whether you stream your news over the internet, watch it on TV, or read it on social media or in a newspaper, be on the lookout for these common types of news:

BREAKING NEWS

Usually reported the same day or the day after a newsworthy event occurs, these stories often answer basic questions—the who, what, where, when, and why of a story. Typically, they include a time reference, such as "yesterday," "today," or "on Tuesday."

NEWS ANALYSIS

These stories provide additional background and more in-depth information. They sometimes use historical information and research to help readers and viewers assess what may come next.

FEATURES

Often more in-depth than breaking news, features tend to include interviews with famous people or report on trends—for example, if school cafeterias are serving healthier food, or bald eagles are making a comeback. Timing can be less important for features.

OPINIONS AND EDITORIALS

Opinion editors, TV presenters, or experts share their perspectives in opinion or editorial pieces. They use research and reporting to build a case to support their opinions.

INVESTIGATIVE JOURNALISM

Through in-depth reporting and original research, journalists reveal information that was previously hidden from, or not commonly known by, the public. These investigative stories are often compiled by teams of reporters and can take days, months, or even years to develop.

DATA JOURNALISM

Data journalists use computer software to gather huge amounts of public information, or data, from governments, police, and other sources. They use the data to reveal important stories, such as increases in certain kinds of crime, and the data can be turned into interactive maps and visuals online or on TV.

Interactive maps are one form of visual journalism. This one shows the average number of tornadoes in the United States each year.

VISUAL JOURNALISM

Similar to data journalism, visual journalism often uses interactive online maps and graphics to enhance stories. This style of reporting also features multimedia storytelling, using videos, photos, virtual reality, and other visuals.

A photojournalist takes photos of police at a 2016 protest in Lima, Peru.

PHOTOJOURNALISM

People post hundreds of photos of news events online almost the second they happen. But true photojournalism is different. Instead of showing pictures of everything that happens, a photojournalist captures one powerful moment that communicates the emotion and importance of a story. These photos often appear in newspapers, magazines, or online.

This 1899 illustration, published in a weekly newspaper in Milan, Italy, offers a historical look at people's never-ending appetite for news.

14

1

The History of NEWS

Today, headlines leap out at us from mobile phones, TV screens, computers, and newspapers everywhere we turn. But long before the internet existed, even before there was electricity, people were hungry for the latest news. What scandals have broken out in the kingdom? Will the village come under attack from invaders? And will that thief who stole from his neighbor be punished? The questions aren't so different today. It's *how* the news travels, how quickly it travels, and whether it spreads throughout a village or to people around the globe that has changed.

Back in ancient Rome, more than 2,000 years ago, people flocked to the town square or to the market to get their news. Rumors and stories, both true and untrue, flew around the stalls as people purchased their daily bread. As early as 59 B.C., Romans who were lucky enough to know how to read could get a daily dose of information from a handwritten gazette, called the *Acta Diurna,* which the Roman government created and posted in public places. A forerunner of the newspaper, the gazette reported on who had won the gladiator contest, what laws had been passed, and even the daily horoscope. But the *Acta Diurna* only shared information that the rulers wanted the public to know.

Unlike common people, Roman emperors and rulers had special ways of getting news from afar. A vast road system had been set up to move troops across their empire, and the roads became equally useful in spreading information. Emperor Augustus, who came to power around 30 B.C., used a network of couriers on horseback who

A statue of Roman emperor Augustus, a ruler who took power around 30 B.C. and had a network of messengers to bring him news

16

Around 1450, German craftsman Johannes Gutenberg patented his first printing press using movable type, which could print 250 pages an hour.

traveled up to 50 miles (80 km) a day. Messengers usually showed up with a written note of introduction from whoever had sent them and then delivered the message by reading it out loud. Understandably, recipients were more likely to believe news that came from a trusted person. Earlier civilizations, such as the Persian Empire—which at its peak stretched from Egypt to the Middle East to India—also had elaborate courier systems, but the Roman Empire had by far the most successful communication system of the time.

Halfway around the world and hundreds of years later, in ancient China, a publication called the *bao* reported on court affairs in the city now called Beijing. The *bao* was published for more than a thousand years, beginning in A.D. 618 and running all the way until 1911, but it was only for educated government employees.

As societies transformed and time marched on, news continued to travel by word of mouth. In the early 1300s, the most trusted news for villagers and rulers alike was still delivered in person. And much like in ancient Rome, powerful European rulers shelled out huge amounts of money to keep a group of trusted messengers who brought them valuable information. The common people would often learn about official announcements from the town crier, whose job it was to wander the streets

An early printing press

shouting the latest news from the royal court. For unofficial news, villagers still gathered in town, often gossiping over food and drink.

THE **Miracle** MACHINE

Around 1450, a new invention changed the way news was delivered, which would slowly change the world. German craftsman Johannes Gutenberg patented his printing press using movable type. The machine consisted of individual metal letters that could be rearranged and reused after a page was printed. Operated by hand, it could print 250 pages an hour—which was much faster than handwriting every sheet. Because of Gutenberg's invention, people gradually began to rely more on the printed word than on a neighbor's gossip.

famous FLUB

SPANISH SURPRISE
In August 1588, a fleet of Spanish warships was beaten in a battle against the English. However, news delivered by three different sources reported that the Spanish had won! People in Spain celebrated and the English mourned for a whole *month* before getting the true story.

17

THE **Birth** OF THE NEWSPAPER

The earliest versions of newspapers started appearing in European cities by the 1500s. These small pamphlets, called newsbooks, were often read aloud in the town square. They contained updates on the latest battles, crimes, and scandals. Across the Atlantic Ocean, some of the first printed news reports started appearing in Mexico City, Mexico, in 1542. Called *hoja volante* (flying sheets), the single-page reports usually covered one news event at a time and were popular throughout the 1600s. The first modern newspaper was published in 1605, in the European city of Strasbourg—on the border of France and Germany.

During the next 25 years, European governments became more established and their citizens began to crave more reliable information. Newspapers sprang up across Europe. By 1665, the *Oxford Gazette* in London, England, had become the first widely read and authoritative newspaper.

But these early newspapers were a complete snooze compared with today's papers. They had no headlines, no pictures, and just a few lines of text for each story. Many were also official government publications, which included only news the government wanted people to see.

The first American colonial newspaper, printed in 1690, was called *Publick*

A 17th-century engraving shows Strasbourg, France, where the first modern newspaper was published.

Occurrences Both Forreign and Domestick. But the paper was shut down after its first issue for failure to obtain the correct printing license, and perhaps for including biting criticisms of the king of France. It was 14 years before another paper would be printed in the Colonies.

Newspapers really started catching on in the 1700s, and by 1775, major cities in the United States—such as New York, Boston, Baltimore, and Philadelphia—were brimming with some 40 newspapers. Originally about four pages long, these papers included a combination of foreign news—mostly reprinted from British papers—along with some local gossip and advertisements. As the American Revolution approached, newspapers became the place to find out about politics, and they helped shift the public toward supporting independence from Britain.

A March 7, 1771, edition of the *Massachusetts Spy* newspaper

What would happen if the U.S. government controlled the press today?

RISE OF THE Scribes

Scribes in ancient Egypt wrote everything out by hand.

Long before machines could print thousands of newspapers an hour, every document on Earth had to be handwritten. In ancient Egypt, specially trained writers, called scribes, wrote everything from marriage contracts to plans for new buildings. Very few people could read and write, so scribes had a high status in society. They also had to be extremely trustworthy, as they often wrote secret letters for kings.

Fast-forward about a thousand years, and scribes were busy at work in Europe. At first, around A.D. 1000, most scribes were monks who mostly copied religious books. In the 1200s, the demand for books became so great that professional scribes started making copies for sale in bookstores. They had to write fast to make a living.

By the 1500s, scribes in bustling Italian cities worked for the ruling class and for businessmen. Some clever scribes gathered all kinds of insider information about everything from business matters to town gossip. They wrote up this valuable information in weekly handwritten reports and quietly sold them to wealthy buyers.

quill and parchment

19

BENJAMIN FRANKLIN
Founding Father of Newspapers
(1706–1790)

Long before Benjamin Franklin became a Founding Father of the United States, he was one of the best journalists in the American Colonies. After working as an apprentice to his older brother, James, who owned Boston's *New-England Courant*, Franklin jumped at the chance to buy the *Pennsylvania Gazette* in 1729. Only the second newspaper ever printed in Philadelphia, the *Gazette* quickly became the most widely read newspaper in the Colonies.

In the years leading up to the American Revolution—in which the American Colonies fought for independence from England from 1775 to 1783—Franklin used the *Gazette* to speak out against the British government. In 1776, Franklin would go on to help draft the Declaration of Independence, a document that declared the Colonies' right to choose their own government and form their own nation.

THE **Need** FOR SPEED

Before long, the world started speeding up. With the introduction of electricity in the late 1800s, the telegraph in 1844, the telephone in 1876, and the expansion of railroads across Europe and the United States throughout the 19th century, news began to travel faster and farther. At the beginning of the century, it would take at least four days for news to be delivered from mainland Europe to England by boat and on horseback and some three weeks for news to travel across the United States. By the end of the century, news could travel around the globe in a matter of minutes.

In 1814, the invention of steam-powered printing presses meant that newspapers could be churned out at a rate of 5,000 copies an hour, and by the middle of the century, some presses were pumping out 18,000 copies an hour. In the middle of the century, reporters embraced the telegraph, which transmitted printed messages by wire across the country and around the world. Suddenly, information was traveling so fast that newspapers competed to be the first to publish major stories.

Until this point, newspapers had been expensive and were mostly read by well-to-do people. But that changed in 1833, when New York printer Benjamin Day published the *New York Sun*, the first "penny paper," which sold for one cent instead of the usual price of six cents. Its stories appealed to a wider audience, with its sizzling accounts of crime, strange happenings, and other human-interest pieces. Within two years, *The Sun* became one of the top-selling newspapers in the world. Soon penny papers were popping up in other major cities.

But newspapers were not only big news in East Coast cities. During the 1800s, they became important sources of information for people across the country and in places that would one day become part of the United States. More than a hundred newspapers were published in New Mexico, Texas, California, and Arizona during the mid to late 1800s. These states were Spanish and Mexican territories before joining the United States in the 1840s, so many of these early papers were printed either in Spanish or in English and Spanish. The California gold rush, which peaked in 1852, brought a flood of people to Northern California from all over the world. And newspapers in a multitude of languages soon popped up to reach these readers.

By the end of the 19th century, the biggest newspapers had nearly a million readers. And they started to look more like today's papers, with photographs, big headlines, comic strips, and sports coverage. Most important, many papers in Europe and the United States could write openly about politics and powerful people. Advertisers were eager to appear on their pages, and newspapers started making a lot of money. News became big business, and the golden age of newspapers had begun.

> ## Four hostile newspapers are to be more dreaded than a hundred thousand bayonets.
>
> —NAPOLEON BONAPARTE (1769–1821)

NICASIO IDAR
A Voice for Mexican Texans
(1855–1914)

Born in Texas only 10 years after the former Mexican territory became a U.S. state, Nicasio Idar grew up to become a newspaper editor and publisher. He was also a pioneer in the fight for the rights of Mexican Texans (Tejanos).

As editor and publisher of *La Crónica*, a Spanish-language newspaper in Laredo, Texas, Idar wrote about the injustices Tejanos faced, including discrimination, segregated schools, poor working conditions, and violent attacks because of their race. He became a leader in the Tejano community, even organizing a conference in 1911 to take action against racial discrimination.

Three of Idar's eight children worked on the newspaper: his daughter Jovita and sons Clemente and Eduardo. They all went on to become journalists and outspoken advocates for equality for women and Mexicans.

Nicasio Idar's daughter, Jovita, and two of her brothers followed in the family newspaper tradition; they are shown here at the *El Progreso* newspaper in 1914.

FREDERICK DOUGLASS
Antislavery Newsmaker
(circa 1818–1895)

Frederick Douglass began life as an enslaved man yet rose to be one of the most important public figures of the U.S. Civil War (1861–65) and the antislavery movement. Douglass believed that learning to read would be his path to freedom. While enslaved, he secretly taught himself and other enslaved people to read—a brave and illegal act. In 1838, Douglass escaped from Maryland, a slave state, to New York City, where slavery was illegal.

From there, Douglass began to travel, stirring up support for the antislavery cause in the United States and Europe. After spending years overseas, he returned to the United States and became a writer for an abolitionist newspaper, which aimed to end slavery. He later bought a printing press and his own paper, called the *North Star*, which was named for the route to freedom used by enslaved persons. They often found their way from south to north by following the North Star. In the years leading up to the U.S. Civil War—when the northern and southern states fought over slavery—the *North Star* became the most important black-owned newspaper in the fight against slavery.

PROSPECTUS
FOR AN ANTI-SLAVERY PAPER, TO BE ENTITLED
NORTH STAR.
FREDERICK DOUGLASS

Proposes to publish, in ROCHESTER, N. Y., a **WEEKLY ANTI-SLAVERY PAPER**, with the above title.

The object of the NORTH STAR will be to attack SLAVERY in all its forms and aspects; advocate UNIVERSAL EMANCIPATION; exalt the standard of PUBLIC MORALITY; promote the Moral and Intellectual Improvement of the COLORED PEOPLE; and hasten the day of FREEDOM to the Three Millions of our ENSLAVED FELLOW COUNTRYMEN.

The Paper will be printed upon a double medium sheet, at $2,00 per annum, if paid in advance, or $2,50, if payment be delayed over six months.

The names of Subscribers may be sent to the following named persons, and should be forwarded, as far as practicable, by the first of November, proximo.

FREDERICK DOUGLASS, Lynn, Mass.
SAMUEL BROOKE, Salem, Ohio.
M. R. DELANY, Pittsburgh, Pa.
VALENTINE NICHOLSON, Harveysburgh, Warren Co. O.
Mr. WALCOTT, 21 Cornhill, Boston.

JOEL P. DAVIS, Economy, Wayne County, Ind.
CHRISTIAN DONALDSON, Cincinnati, Ohio.
J. M'KIM, Philadelphia, Pa.
AMARANCY PAINE, Providence, R. I.
Mr. GAY, 142 Nassau Street, New York.

JOSEPH PULITZER
News Pioneer and Stunt Man
(1847–1911)

One of the fathers of the modern newspaper, Joseph Pulitzer gained fame and fortune as the owner and publisher of the *New York World* newspaper. He printed gripping stories about dishonesty and crimes committed by people in power. Pulitzer was also one of the first to include illustrations as well as comics, sports coverage, and fashion in newspapers.

The newspaperman drummed up publicity by running sizzling headlines and staging wild news stunts. In one such instance, he raised $100,000 in donations from readers to build a pedestal for the Statue of Liberty—a recent gift from France. He published the name of every donor, and of course, they all bought the paper so they could see their name in print. Within 10 years after its first issue, the *World* had more than 600,000 readers. It had become the largest newspaper in the country.

From 1896 to 1898, Pulitzer and New York's other famous newsman, William Randolph Hearst, who ran the *New York Morning Journal,* were locked in an epic battle for readers. The two papers raced to outdo each other, with each headline and stunt crazier than the next. This style of sensational and shocking news became known as "yellow journalism." Pulitzer eventually pulled back from the battle, instead focusing on serious investigations in the pages of the *World*.

Before Pulitzer died, he set aside money to create the Columbia University School of Journalism in New York City—still one of the nation's top journalism schools. He also funded the Pulitzer Prize, one of today's most respected awards in American journalism.

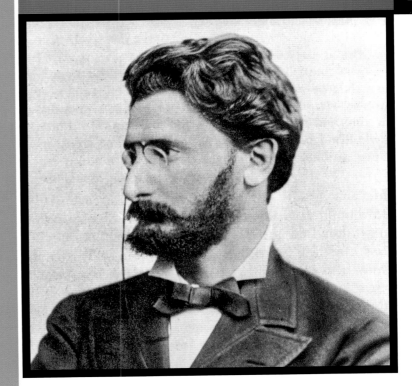

CHANGE IN Delivery

In the early 1900s, a new style of journalism—called investigative reporting—swept the country, aiming to expose corrupt businessmen and government officials. Papers that published these important, true stories had to compete with a wave of yellow journalism meant to attract more readers with shocking, even scandalous stories. Eventually, readers grew tired of one corruption scandal after another. Advertisers also became skittish, pulling out of publications with these controversial pieces, which forced newspapers to stop publishing the stories or shut down. But the serious investigative reports helped launch modern-day journalism, and ultimately, newspaper readership continued to grow.

The public's hunger for news seemed unstoppable. A New York publisher named Henry Luce believed that news had become too local. To help make it more global, he launched *Time* magazine in 1923, publishing short news articles from around the globe. He went on to expand his empire, launching the business magazine *Fortune* and the photography magazine *Life*. News magazines caught on, and competitors such as *Newsweek* arrived on the scene. At the same time, new technology made it possible to print in color, opening up the age of the "picture magazine." Modern cameras were now small enough for photographers to carry them everywhere, bringing images of the world back to readers in their living rooms. In 1914, *National Geographic* magazine printed the first natural color photograph in its pages, and in 1935, the magazine became a pioneer in the use of color photography.

National Geographic published its first photograph taken by a female photographer, Eliza Scidmore, in the July 4, 1914, issue, shown here.

NELLIE BLY
Daredevil Reporter
(1864–1922)

The incredible reporting stunts of Nellie Bly—born Elizabeth Jane Cochrane—would be newsworthy even today. But they were especially incredible in the late 1800s, when few newspapers would ever consider hiring a female reporter. Bly had grown bored of writing about gardening tips and recipes for a newspaper in Pennsylvania. She moved to New York, determined to make a name for herself. In her first story for the *New York World*, Bly posed as someone with mental illness to get committed to a hospital. Her shocking stories about how the patients were treated made her instantly famous.

In 1889, she cooked up a story that would become a worldwide sensation. Inspired by Jules Verne's famous novel *Around the World in Eighty Days*, Bly challenged herself to beat the fictional "record" set by the book's lead character. In the days before airplanes, she pledged to travel around the world in less than 80 days! Traveling by ship, train, horse, donkey, and any other means necessary, Bly completed her journey in 72 days, 6 hours, 11 minutes, and 14 seconds—setting a new world record. Her brave stunts made her famous, but many also consider her the founder of investigative journalism.

THE World LISTENS

The public loved print newspapers and magazines, but radio was about to offer news in a way people could have never dreamed. In the 1920s, radio stations debuted with entertaining shows that families tuned in to every night. For the very first time, news could be reported as it happened. By the time the United States entered World War II in 1941, radio networks had reporters on the ground in Europe. Americans listening to their radios at home could hear the sounds of bombs going off in the background, soldiers' boots slogging through mud, and firsthand accounts of soldiers' experiences during the war.

From 1930 through the 1940s—the golden age of radio—many families would listen to radio shows together for entertainment.

EDWARD R. MURROW
Father of Broadcast News
(1908–1965)

Radio was still new in 1939 when Edward R. Murrow was sent to Europe to record radio reports. Murrow and his team became some of America's first foreign news correspondents. When World War II broke out, he made daily reports from London, England, for listeners back in New York. But instead of stiffly reporting the news like most announcers, Murrow would stand on rooftops to capture the sounds of air raid sirens. Down on the ground, he'd place his microphone on the sidewalk so listeners could hear the shuffle of pedestrians' feet as they rushed into bomb shelters. His reports brought the war into people's living rooms, leading many Americans to support U.S. entry into the conflict.

By the time Murrow returned to the United States after the war, he had become a star. Television was brand-new and, in 1951, Murrow jumped into that, too. In 1954, he made history when he used his TV show to speak out against Senator Joseph McCarthy, who threatened and harassed people he suspected were Communists (an enemy political party at the time)—though the senator had no evidence to back up his claims.

Murrow made his mark on journalism in many ways. A pioneer of broadcast journalism, Murrow still influences those in the industry today.

By the mid-1950s, music ruled the radio airwaves. Newly invented transistor radios allowed people to carry their tunes wherever they went.

23

On June 1, 1953, a crowd in New York City watches the coronation of Queen Elizabeth II on a TV displayed in a store window.

AMERICA GETS Hooked ON TV

Americans' love affair with radio would not last long before it was challenged by a new fascination: television. Today, it's hard to imagine never having seen news as it was happening across town or around the world, but in the late 1940s, the only moving pictures many people had seen were movies. Now the whole country was awestruck. Crowds would gather around televisions displayed in store windows to watch their favorite sports or other big events. In 1950, almost no one had a television at home, but by 1955, nearly half of American homes had TVs.

Broadcast news at that time was not very exciting by today's standards. Now, news programs might have several presenters and cut away to journalists reporting "live from scene" as events unfold. But back in the 1950s, one presenter would sit in front of the camera for the whole program and read the news—there was no fancy video, not even a weatherperson. Other TV shows that were just for entertainment used costumes and backdrops like the theater. Americans fell in love with programs like *I Love Lucy* and *The Lone Ranger*, and saw rock legend Elvis perform on TV for the first time. And Americans had very few channels back then, unlike the dozens of shows we have today, so everyone watched the same shows and news programs.

ABOVE: Although already a hit on the radio and in film, the Lone Ranger became even more popular when he and his trusty horse, Silver, galloped over to television in 1949. LEFT: Vivian Vance and Lucille Ball star in the 1950s hit TV comedy *I Love Lucy*.

As anchor of the *CBS Evening News* (1962–1981), Walter Cronkite helped shape the face of television news. In polls, people often ranked him as the most trusted man in America.

ALL News ALL THE TIME

In the late 1960s, Americans started swapping their black-and-white TVs for color ones. Reporting of the news started moving faster. The invention of communications satellites in the 1960s meant that news could be "beamed" directly to networks and stations, without having to be prerecorded on tapes that were hand-delivered to the networks. For the first time, journalists could report from "live trucks," which used special technology to send news back to the station as it was happening.

For decades, news networks were the kings of television. In the 1970s, 90 percent of viewers tuned in to the "big three"—ABC, NBC, and CBS—to watch the nightly news and their favorite shows. But when cable television arrived in the 1980s,

Americans had even more options. CNN became the first 24-hour cable news channel, capturing global events before anyone else. As other cable news channels launched, such as MSNBC and Fox News Channel, competition among news outlets—TV and newspapers alike—became fiercer than ever. The race to get the scoop became a 24-hour marathon instead of a sprint to the next morning's paper or the opening broadcast of the nightly news. And with so much competition, some

networks set themselves apart by tailoring their content to people with strong political views—MSNBC now appeals to more liberal viewers, while Fox News Channel appeals to a more conservative audience.

Television news vans contain all the technology needed to produce a live broadcast from the field.

HEY, THAT'S A HOAX! **SUPERSIZED** SPUD

Back in 1894, a potato farmer in Loveland, Colorado, U.S.A., created one of the first fake viral photos. The farmer posed for a picture holding a potato the size of a boulder—which he claimed measured more than two feet (0.6 m) long and weighed some 86 pounds (39 kg)! Or at least that's what it *looked* like. The gargantuan spud was actually a picture of a normal-size potato enlarged to huge proportions and pasted to a piece of board.

The fake photo was intended to be a funny advertisement, but once copies of the picture got out, this potato prank just kept on rolling. In 1895, the photo fell into the hands of editors at *Scientific American,* who published a serious news story about the amazing giant spud. They quickly discovered it was a fake and printed a retraction—a statement explaining that an earlier story was incorrect. But the story kept going. Over the next several years, the phony potato showed up in many newspapers and magazines. And the legend lives on. The massive vegetable was featured in a 2012 play called *The Great Loveland*

Potato Hoax. It turns out, hoax photos have been "going viral" for centuries—but at a much slower pace than today.

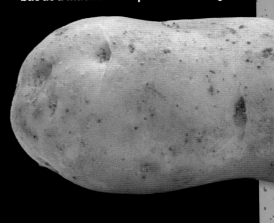

What do you think will be the next big invention that will change the way we get news?

THE INTERNET IS THE NEW **Village Square**

With all the changes in the news media over the last two centuries, nothing turned journalism upside down quite like the internet. Today, anyone with a computer can blog or post articles online that look like news; anyone with a cell phone can be a photographer or cameraperson; and people around the world can post images of events as they happen, before the professional news organizations even know about them.

In some ways, the internet is like the market in the village square of the 1400s. Except the latest news and gossip aren't limited to a tiny village. Instead, they travel around the world in seconds. And we don't always know who is delivering our online news. So figuring out which sources to trust can be difficult.

Media *Makes* History

When important stories break, whether they are terrible or uplifting, the media has the power to connect people from all over the world. These historic events marked major changes in the way journalists reported news and the way audiences consumed it.

THE SINKING OF THE *TITANIC*

April 15, 1912

The R.M.S. *Titanic*, the "unsinkable" ocean liner, had struck an iceberg on its very first voyage. Reporters called emergency rescue operators to find out what was happening. But in the confusion, only snippets of information came through. The facts were uncertain, and the fate of the passengers was unknown. In one embarrassing story, radio operators confused the *Titanic* with another ship, telling reporters that everyone on board was safe. The headline in London's *Daily Mail* the next day read, "No lives lost."

The *New York Times*, however, checked multiple sources, instead of relying on just one. And the paper was the first to get the story right. The morning after the accident, it reported that the *Titanic* had sunk, while other papers were still saying that the fate of the ship was unknown. The *Times* continued to beat other reporters to the story as it unfolded throughout the week. From that day forward, the *Times* became New York's leading newspaper and still is today. The way the story was covered also set a new standard for how the media would handle future disasters—committing full resources to a major story and racing to be the first to be published.

TV'S FIRST PRESIDENTIAL DEBATE

September 26, 1960

Presidential candidates John F. Kennedy and Richard M. Nixon squared off in the first televised U.S. presidential debate in history. By 1960, most American homes had televisions, and some 70 million viewers tuned in to watch. At the time, that was the most people ever to have watched a single program.

Nixon entered the debate with a slight lead in the race, but all of that changed when the handsome and well-dressed Kennedy walked onto the stage. In contrast, Nixon was recovering from the flu and was running a fever. He appeared pale, sweaty, and like he had forgotten to shave. Kennedy looked directly into the camera as he gave answers, while Nixon tended to look off to the side.

After the debate, polls showed that people who had listened to the debate on the radio thought that Nixon had won, whereas people who watched the debate on TV thought Kennedy had. Many people believe that Kennedy beat Nixon in the election because he looked better on television. After this debate, no one could deny the power of television in shaping public opinion.

QUEEN ELIZABETH II'S CORONATION

June 2, 1953

When Britain's Princess Elizabeth was crowned queen, it was huge news in the United Kingdom and around the world. The elaborate ceremony was the first coronation to be televised and the world's first international television event. People stopped whatever they were doing to watch; some threw viewing parties. In the end, 27 million people in the U.K. tuned in, as well as millions more around the globe, a remarkable number given that many households didn't even have TVs yet. The event helped establish television as a new form of mass media.

THE WATERGATE SCANDAL

1972-74

Two young *Washington Post* reporters, Bob Woodward and Carl Bernstein, were assigned to cover a break-in at the Democratic National Committee (DNC) headquarters in the Watergate office building in Washington, D.C. On the night of the break-in, five people were arrested with suspicious tools, thousands of dollars in cash, and listening devices that could be used to bug the DNC office.

Woodward and Bernstein wrote a series of stories that linked the burglars closer and closer to President Richard M. Nixon. An anonymous source led the reporters to discover that senior officials in the White House had been involved in planning the break-in and that the president himself may have directed the burglary. In 1974, a White House recording revealed Nixon had been involved in covering up the crime. While facing impeachment by Congress, the president resigned from office. Woodward and Bernstein inspired a whole generation of investigative journalists to hold government officials accountable for their actions.

This photo, sent (from Mars!) by NASA's Phoenix Mars Lander, confirmed that there is ice on the red planet. The lumps of ice are on the lower left side of the photo.

> **MarsPhoenix** ✔
> @MarsPhoenix
>
> Are you ready to celebrate? Well, get ready: We have ICE!!!!! Yes, ICE, *WATER ICE* on Mars! w00t!!! Best day ever!!
>
> ♡ 914 7:14 PM - Jun 19, 2008   ⓘ
>
> 💬 168 people are talking about this   ›

A ROBOT TWEETS

June 19, 2008

"Are you ready to celebrate? Well, get ready: We have ICE!!!!! Yes, ICE, *WATER ICE* on Mars! w00t!!" The Twitter account of NASA's robot known as the Phoenix Mars Lander revealed this astounding news to the world. The robot had landed safely on Mars and used a robotic arm to scoop up samples of Martian soil. After performing tests on the sample, the robot confirmed for the first time what scientists had long suspected—there is ice on Mars! All life on Earth requires water to live. Scientists are betting that the same goes for life on Mars. So finding frozen water on the red planet was a huge first step in figuring out if life has ever existed there.

OK, so a real person on Earth was behind the robot's Twitter account, but it was still a big deal that NASA broke the news on Twitter hours before it was reported on TV or on internet news sites. Twitter was becoming a more direct, and less formal, way to communicate with the public—even for NASA and other government agencies.

PRESIDENT BARACK OBAMA'S INAUGURATION

January 20, 2009

The historic election of Barack Obama as the first African-American president of the United States drew more than a million people to Washington, D.C., to watch the inauguration—the ceremony where the new president is sworn into office. But millions more were watching the event live on their computer screens.

Obama was the first president elected since streaming technology became widely available to the public. Many television networks and news websites streamed the event. CNN even partnered with Facebook, so the TV network could show people's posts about the ceremony as it happened. As this book goes to press, the inauguration holds the record for the most livestreamed event in U.S. history, with internet traffic hitting its highest peak ever during Obama's speech. If anyone had doubts, that day showed that livestreaming would play a major role in the future of how people get their news.

Dr. Martin Luther King, Jr., gives his historic "I Have a Dream" speech at the 1963 March on Washington.

? Have you ever watched a video or TV news story that helped you understand someone else's point of view?

32

HOW **TV** CHANGED THE
CIVIL RIGHTS MOVEMENT

During the African-American civil rights movement of the 1950s and '60s, **black people protested to demand rights equal to those of white people. A leader of this movement, Martin Luther King, Jr., preached the importance of peaceful protests. The police, however, often used violence or arrested activists while television cameras rolled. Television was still new, so for the first time, people of all races were able to see with their own eyes what was happening across the United States.**

These events, some shown on the following page, captured the world's attention and helped build support for passage of two important laws: the Civil Rights Act of 1964, which made all segregation illegal, and the Voting Rights Act of 1965, which outlawed fees and reading tests for voters. The law also made it illegal to stop people from voting because of their race. Both laws were a huge step forward for all people of color, including African Americans, Hispanics, Native Americans, and others who faced frequent discrimination.

MONTGOMERY BUS BOYCOTT
Montgomery, Alabama, 1955–56

African-American newspapers jumped on the story of Rosa Parks, the black woman who was arrested after refusing to give up her seat to a white man on a bus. Her arrest set off a boycott that lasted more than a year, in which African Americans refused to ride city buses. The white-run, mainstream media—which were the largest newspapers and TV networks with the biggest audiences—were slow to catch on. But when Martin Luther King, Jr., was arrested for protesting, these larger media outlets started covering the boycott, which meant that people from all backgrounds became aware of the protests. The fight to end segregation started gaining widespread support among the American public. In 1956, the U.S. Supreme Court ruled that laws to keep buses segregated were illegal.

THE LITTLE ROCK NINE
Little Rock, Arkansas, September 4, 1957

When the "Little Rock Nine," a group of African-American students, arrived for their first day at a previously all-white high school in Arkansas, news cameras were rolling. The nation watched as this group of kids tested the law that said schools could no longer be segregated. People saw not only the group of white people who shouted and threw things at the teenagers, but also the expressions on the students' faces, and the Arkansas National Guard trying to stop black students from entering the school. Later that month, the students returned to the school, protected by U.S. soldiers sent by President Dwight D. Eisenhower. Media in the United States and around the world followed the story closely.

THE MARCH ON WASHINGTON
Washington, D.C., August 28, 1963

Civil rights leader Martin Luther King, Jr., gave his now famous "I Have a Dream" speech to 250,000 people who marched on Washington, D.C., to demand equal rights for African Americans. Two TV networks ran live coverage of the entire march, broadcasting across the country and around the globe. Before the march, newspapers and local TV stations outside of major cities had barely covered the civil rights movement or only presented one point of view. The television broadcast of the march allowed African Americans to tell their stories straight to the American public and to the world. It also allowed viewers to see the size of the crowd supporting King and how the civil rights leader delivered his strong but peaceful message. King's powerful speech got exposure from media to raise awareness and help boost support for laws that ended segregation and protected African Americans' right to vote. When King was assassinated in 1968, the tragedy set off a wave of riots and violence in a hundred cities across the United States.

BLOODY SUNDAY
Selma, Alabama, March 7, 1965

State troopers attacked the more than 600 people—mostly African Americans—peacefully marching from Selma, Alabama, to the state capital. The news media were there to capture images of law enforcement using tear gas and billy clubs on innocent people. Television news broadcast the images across the nation, and support for the civil rights movement grew.

"If it hadn't been for the media, the civil rights movement would have been like a bird without wings..."
—JOHN LEWIS, CONGRESSMAN AND LEADER OF THE SELMA MARCH

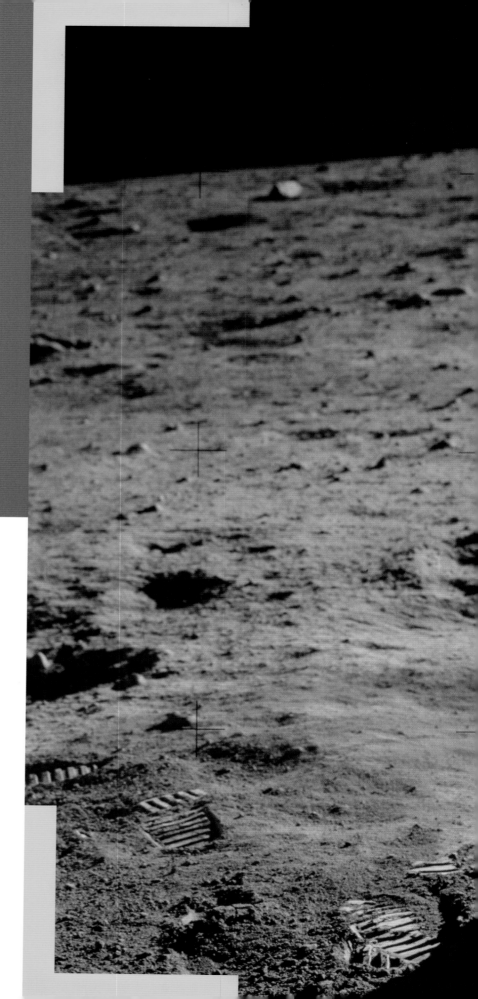

MOON WALKER

A photograph can add to a story, by showing something more to readers. Sometimes a photograph can have a greater impact than any written report. Every now and then, like magic, a photographer captures an image that lives beyond the pages of today's news and will be remembered for decades and maybe even centuries.

34

Millions of Earthlings were glued to their television sets on July 20, 1969, as astronauts Neil Armstrong and Buzz Aldrin became the first humans to walk on the moon. People had seen grainy telescope-like photographs of the moon before, but they certainly had not ever seen it like this—with a human on it! The whole world watched the events broadcast live, but this simple photograph of astronaut Buzz Aldrin standing on the moon captured the country's hopes, dreams, pride, and awe at this remarkable human achievement. It was the first still image of a human on a distant world. If you look closely, you can see Neil Armstrong, the photographer, reflected in Aldrin's visor.

Riot police—armed with tear gas, rubber bullets, and a water cannon—stand at the ready as this TV reporter prepares to deliver a live broadcast in September 2019 during a demonstration in Hong Kong.

2

Making the NEWS

Journalism has the power to educate the public, to sway opinions, and, sometimes, to change the world. But because of this power, journalists are often at risk—and many have put their lives on the line to tell important stories. Journalists in the United States and many other democratic countries are lucky to have tremendous freedom. For example, they can travel the world and be the first to learn about a major discovery, interview a leader, or cover wars and natural disasters.

FREEDOM OF Speech

Over the years, the press has fought hard for its freedom in courts of law. Why do they go to such great lengths? Because the freedom of all citizens depends on the media's right to expose wrongdoing or bad behavior, hold the powerful accountable, and keep the public informed.

THE FIRST AMENDMENT

In the United States, every video you watch, every speech you hear, and every story you read is protected by one sentence in the U.S. Constitution called the First Amendment. Part of the Bill of Rights, the First Amendment guarantees freedom of speech and freedom of the press. Believe it or not, this single amendment protects your right to say nearly whatever you want. It also allows newspapers, websites, TV networks, and radio stations to publish or broadcast almost any information they want, with very few limitations. And it protects the media's role as "watchdogs." That means journalists can publish stories about powerful people who do dishonest things. And they can do so without fear of censorship—the government blocking stories it doesn't like from being published. With this freedom comes great responsibility for journalists to ensure their reporting is accurate and that controversial stories are handled with sensitivity.

FOUNDERS Fight FOR A FREE PRESS

At the time of the American Revolution (1775–1783) and during the period the Founding Fathers were drafting the U.S. Constitution (1787), newspapers were not expected to be objective. That means it was OK for them to write about only one side of an argument; they didn't have to tell multiple sides of a story. Writers often lashed out at public figures, hurling insults at them. But even though the Founding Fathers faced this harsh criticism, they understood the importance of an unrestricted press. They believed it would ensure the United States would remain a free country in the future.

When Founding Father and future U.S. president James Madison proposed the First Amendment, he said that the freedom of the press, as one of the great protectors of liberty, should be fiercely defended.

THE RIGHT TO **Write**

Over the centuries, freedom of the press has faced many challenges. Only a few years after the First Amendment was ratified, President John Adams signed the Sedition Act of 1798, which made it legal to fine or jail editors who printed "any false, scandalous and malicious writing ... against the government of the United States." Many editors went to prison as punishment for speaking out against the government. The law turned out to be unpopular with many people and was allowed to expire in 1801. Later, in the 1820s and '30s, some southern states passed new laws making anti-slavery newspapers illegal. Today, these laws would be considered violations of the First Amendment.

One of the biggest challenges to the First Amendment took place in 1971, during the Vietnam War, when a U.S. government official leaked an embarrassing and damaging report, which was first written about in the *New York Times.* Known as the Pentagon Papers, the report revealed that during the long war, several U.S. presidents had misled the public about the level of U.S. involvement in the conflict. When the government tried to prevent further stories from being published, the *New York Times* and the *Washington Post* challenged the government in court. The U.S. Supreme Court ruled in favor of the newspapers in a landmark decision, saying the First Amendment protected their right to publish.

After winning a U.S. Supreme Court case over freedom of the press, the *New York Times* continued its coverage of the secret Pentagon Papers in its July 1, 1971, edition.

39

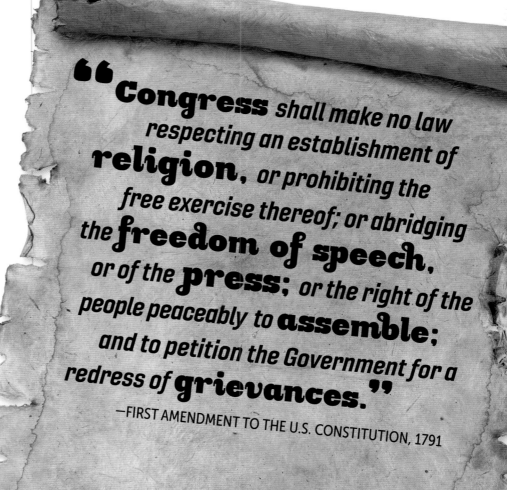

"**Congress** shall make no law respecting an establishment of **religion**, or prohibiting the free exercise thereof; or abridging the **freedom of speech**, or of the **press**; or the right of the people peaceably to **assemble**; and to petition the Government for a redress of **grievances.**"

—FIRST AMENDMENT TO THE U.S. CONSTITUTION, 1791

FREEDOM UNDER **Fire**

Freedom of the press exists in most countries with democratic governments. But in many nondemocratic countries, the government controls the press, and journalists who don't report what the government wants can face harsh punishments. A recent study found that only 13 percent of the world's population has a free press—mostly in western Europe, the United States, Canada, Australia, New Zealand, Japan, and a few Central and South American countries.

In many other countries, saying negative things about government leaders is illegal. Some nations even monitor journalists' emails and internet searches to make sure they are following these strict rules. In Singapore, you are not allowed to insult the courts. In North Korea, one of the world's most restrictive regimes, the country's government owns all media, and journalists can report only positive information about government leaders. Radios and TV sets are preset to government stations, and radios must be checked and registered with the police. Even smartphones don't have access to the internet or unregulated Wi-Fi.

In North Korea's capital, Pyongyang—where media are strictly controlled by the government— a 2017 news report announces the country's advances in nuclear weaponry.

> **"** *Show me a country with* **no free press,** *and you will be showing me a country where* **human rights** *are not respected.* **"**
> —RICHARD GOLDSTONE, SOUTH AFRICAN JUDGE

 famous **FLUB**

DEWEY BEATS TRUMAN

In one of the most famous media mess-ups of all time, the headline in the *Chicago Daily Tribune* announced the wrong winner of the U.S. presidential election of 1948. Everyone thought that Democratic president Harry Truman didn't stand a chance of winning a second term. Polls showed that his opponent, Republican Thomas E. Dewey, was unstoppable. On election night, a newspaper strike forced the *Tribune* to go to press before all the votes were counted. The paper's editors were so confident that Dewey would win that they published the headline, "Dewey Beats Truman." But the next morning, Truman had won the election, and the newspaper was embarrassed. During his presidency, Truman had a rocky relationship with the press and delighted in rubbing the paper's mistake in its face. In this famous photo at left, Truman gleefully displays the false headline.

IN **CHINA,** WHERE SOCIAL MEDIA IS **CENSORED,** PEOPLE OFTEN SHARE RIDDLES THAT CRITICIZE THE GOVERNMENT—A SORT OF **"CODE,"** *SO THEY WON'T BE* **DETECTED.**

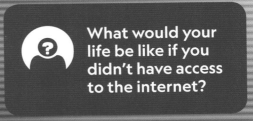

? What would your life be like if you didn't have access to the internet?

WHAT THE U.S. *PRESS CANNOT* SAY

The First Amendment allows the press in the United States to say, print, or broadcast almost anything, but there are some limits. Some types of statements could get reporters into legal trouble, depending on the circumstances. But it often takes a court of law to determine if the speaker or journalist has violated legal standards. So, what language is *not* protected by the First Amendment?

DEFAMATION

A false statement that harms a person's reputation or ability to work can be defamatory. For example, a newspaper cannot accuse someone of wrongdoing, such as a crime, without proof. Imagine if that person were innocent: He could lose his job and his family, or suffer financial hardship, all because of an untrue story. That's why reporters will always say the "alleged thief" or the "alleged hacker," until a suspect is convicted in court and any charges can be attributed to law enforcement officials or court documents. Defamation usually applies only to false statements made with "reckless disregard for the truth." It does not usually apply to opinions. And it is harder for public figures to prove they have been defamed than private people. So expressing a negative opinion about a politician or another famous person is not usually considered defamation.

LIBEL

A defamatory statement made in writing, pictures, or any other physical form is libel (for example, if a journalist writes a story that identifies the wrong person as a crime suspect or victim).

SLANDER

Slander is a defamatory statement that is spoken. This applies to TV and radio news as well as to videos, podcasts, and even speeches.

PLAGIARISM

Publishing someone else's text, photographs, videos, or any other copyrighted material without permission or attribution is called plagiarism. Journalists and the general public cannot publish work legally owned by other people or organizations without getting their permission first.

"FIGHTING WORDS"

Statements that could cause other people to commit illegal or violent acts, or that could cause direct harm to others are called fighting words. Each case is different, and courts do not often agree on the meaning of "fighting words." But some cases that have been debated in the past include yelling insults and swear words in someone's face or encouraging a crowd, such as a group of protesters, to commit violent acts. The First Amendment also does not protect other kinds of language that could cause harm, such as yelling "Fire!" in a theater when there is no fire—people could get hurt in the panic to leave the theater.

A **Push-Pull** RELATIONSHIP

Although the press and government leaders don't always get along in democratic countries, the fact that they can have open, public debates is important to preserving freedom. Even the first U.S. president, George Washington, complained about the press, calling them "infamous scribblers." At the same time, politicians and public figures knew they needed the press to reach the public. Social media has changed this relationship somewhat, as politicians can use it to speak directly to the public, without going through the press. But the First Amendment allows journalists (and the public) to report on or respond freely to leaders' comments on social media as well. Although the Founding Fathers could never have imagined today's technology, this push and pull between public figures and the press is exactly what they intended when they wrote the First Amendment, and this relationship helps keep the United States and other democracies free.

Social media can help political candidates communicate with the public, such as when former Texas congressman Beto O'Rourke (in the blue shirt above) kicked off his 2020 presidential campaign.

CENSORED

THROUGHOUT RECORDED HISTORY, GOVERNMENTS HAVE TRIED TO STOP THE SPREAD OF IDEAS AND PICTURES THEY THINK ARE IN BAD TASTE OR A THREAT TO SOCIETY. YOU MAY BE SURPRISED BY SOME OF THE BOOKS AND MOVIES THAT HAVE BEEN CENSORED IN THE PAST.

1632: Famous Italian astronomer Galileo Galilei started a scandal when he wrote about his theory that Earth revolves around the sun. At that time, the Catholic Church taught that Earth was the center of the universe. Galileo was right, but the church put him under house arrest for the last 10 years of his life.

1929: The Soviet Union (parts of which are now Russia) banned the book *The Adventures of Sherlock Holmes,* by Sir Arthur Conan Doyle, because it contained stories about witchcraft.

1931: The classic children's book *Alice in Wonderland,* by Lewis Carroll, was banned in part of China because it included talking animals and made humans and animals look like equals.

1931: The U.S. state of Ohio banned certain Disney movies because they showed large udders on cartoon cows.

1983: The Alabama State Textbook Committee, in the United States, banned *Anne Frank: The Diary of a Young Girl,* the real diary of a Jewish girl who lived in hiding during the Holocaust—when millions of Jews were killed—because they thought it was a "downer."

2017: The movie *Wonder Woman* was banned in the country of Lebanon because the star of the movie, Gal Gadot, once served in the Israeli Army. Lebanon considers Israel an enemy state.

LET THE INSULTS *FLY*

If a farmer in the ancient Greek city of Athens wanted to complain about the price of bread or express his concerns about a distant war, he had the right to stand before the assembly—the governing body—and speak his mind. The Greeks called this type of free speech *isegoria*, meaning "equal speech in public." This freedom was unique at the time because it applied to all adult males, not only to members of the upper class. That meant peasants, slaves, and the wealthy alike could state their opinions. However, speakers also risked being shouted at or dragged from the podium by fellow citizens who disagreed with them!

Isegoria protected political speech, but Athenian law also protected everyday speech, called *parrhesia*, meaning "to speak openly." Parrhesia described casual conversations in the town market as well as written words, theater performances, and more. And Athenians did not hold back on using this right. They took great pleasure in insulting one another and mocking their leaders—something that would have been punished by death in other societies of the time.

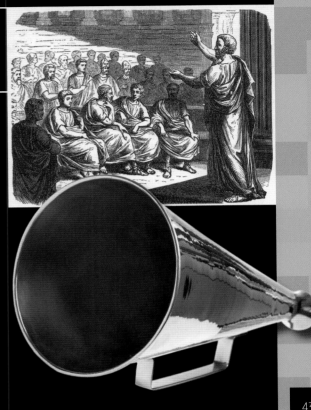

43

" *To* **suppress** *free speech is a* **double wrong.** *It violates the rights of the hearer as well as those of the speaker.* **"**

—FREDERICK DOUGLASS, 1860

GETTING THE Story

Reporters in the United States may have a lot of freedom, but that doesn't mean their jobs are easy. While some report information from a newsroom, their local communities, or the halls of government, others put themselves in dangerous situations to bring stories to people at home. Tornadoes, earthquakes, wildfires, wars, and protests are some of the most challenging stories to cover. To report on these, journalists have to stay safe, which takes skill and preparation. Harder still may be finding the facts during these chaotic events.

GOING TO War

Reporting from war zones is one of the most dangerous jobs journalists can do. Just surviving can be hard enough, but getting to the truth in war zones can be even more challenging. Each side may tell reporters only the information it wants the public to hear. "They try to misuse journalists for their needs," writes veteran war reporter Kurt Pelda, in a report published by a German organization called Konrad-Adenauer-Stiftung. But building trust with sources and knowing a region well can help journalists sniff out a fake story. The best proof, Pelda writes, is seeing with your own eyes.

War reporters also have to be prepared for just about anything. They wear body armor and protective helmets. They carry medical and survival equipment. Newspapers often train war reporters in first aid and battlefield medicine in case their crew is caught in the cross fire during a conflict.

These journalists also need a lot of inside knowledge to stay safe. If journalists are in the line of fire, they need to know what weapons are being used so they can tell which structures will provide enough protection. Can they hide behind a wall or inside a car, or do they need to be inside a stone house? In places where journalists' cell phones are tapped, they may need to plant false phone messages to ward off being detected. And they sometimes have to travel in disguise to avoid being kidnapped or attacked.

War reporters go to great lengths to get the story right—often hiring local journalists to translate and help them with local sources. Reliable information is hard to come by in a war zone, so these reporters have to be extra careful to avoid making mistakes.

Journalists sometimes ride in armored trucks like this one for protection in war zones.

Photojournalist Zohara Bensemra (left) is shown here with a local guide. She helped show the world the damage incurred in Misrata, Libya, during the country's 2011 civil war.

MARIE COLVIN
Witness to War
(1956–2012)

One of the most daring war reporters in history, Marie Colvin was known for placing herself in harm's way—in places where most Western reporters would not go. Born in New York, U.S.A., she reported for the *Sunday Times* newspaper in London, England, for most of her career. Her travels took her to some of the world's most dangerous war zones, where she told the stories of the victims of war—especially women and children—often living side by side with them to learn about their experiences.

While reporting in the Asian country of Sri Lanka in 2001, Colvin came under fire in a grenade attack and was blinded in her left eye. Following that, she became known for wearing a black eye patch. A risk-taker to the end, Colvin was killed in the Middle Eastern country of Syria in 2012, when the Syrian government attacked the media center in the city of Homs where reporters were staying.

ON THE **Home** FRONT

Not all threats to journalists happen far from home. According to the Committee to Protect Journalists, the most dangerous place for reporters to be in the United States is at a protest. When crowds get rowdy and out of control, it's easy for reporters to get caught up in the confusion. In the United States in 2017, at least 20 journalists were arrested, often because they followed protesters who blocked a street or crossed onto private property. That same year, 21 reporters were physically attacked for many reasons. In one case, police used rubber bullets to control a crowd; in others, bystanders assaulted reporters simply because they didn't like the press.

A news reporter conducts an interview at an immigration rights protest in Miami, Florida, U.S.A. Protests can be risky assignments for reporters if crowds get out of control.

EDWARD BRADLEY
War Reporter and Trailblazer
(1941–2006)

Ed Bradley first made a name for himself reporting from war zones for CBS News. In 1973, while reporting in Cambodia, a mortar shell exploded next to him, blowing him into the air. Fragments of the shell struck him in the arm and the back. He escaped with only minor wounds, but he was a lucky man. Just minutes earlier, he had been standing in the exact spot where the shell landed.

Bradley became CBS's first African-American White House correspondent and the first African-American anchor of the *CBS Sunday Night News,* from 1976 to 1981. His talent and popularity helped open doors for future African-American journalists.

Ed Bradley went on to become one of the most famous journalists in America as a correspondent for the popular TV show *60 Minutes,* which he joined in 1981, delivering investigative reports and celebrity interviews for the next 26 years.

A weather reporter and her camera crew battle the strong winds caused by Hurricane Irma in 2017.

HUMANS
VERSUS
Nature

Roofs peel off homes, streets flood, trees tumble over. No one should be outside in a hurricane like this, right? But around the world, reporters and camera crews brave Mother Nature to broadcast reports of extreme weather. So, how do these storm reporters keep themselves safe?

Reporters stand out in the middle of the storm on camera, but what you don't see is that they are usually close to shelter. That way, they can jump back inside if things get out of control.

Reporters must stay safe and also be self-sufficient, which means they need to avoid using emergency services meant for local residents. For example, they come prepared with their own hurricane survival kits, including plenty of dry clothes, food, bottled water, batteries, flashlights, fuel, first aid kits, baby wipes (in case they cannot shower), a satellite phone (for when cell phone communication is cut off), and even their own silverware.

Despite howling winds and driving rain, journalists still have to get the story. So as soon as the worst of the storm blows through, they start interviewing city officials: How bad is the damage? Were people injured? How many homes were lost? They also fan out to talk to local residents, jotting down notes the whole time. Then they turn these interviews into stories.

Media UNDER ATTACK

When government officials use fiery language or pass laws attacking the press, journalists' jobs can become more dangerous. This has happened many times in history. During World War I, U.S. president Woodrow Wilson passed a law making it illegal to say or print anything that was critical of the federal government. One reporter was sentenced to 10 years in prison for publishing articles that claimed the United States had entered the war to benefit financial investors. U.S. president Richard M. Nixon, who served from 1969 to 1974, told his staff, "The press is the enemy." During his time in office, 56 members of the press appeared on his "enemies list," and his staff tried to scare and even arrest some reporters.

U.S. president Barack Obama, who served from 2009 to 2017, spoke out in favor of freedom of the press, but under his government, eight people were charged for leaking news to the media—more than under all previous administrations combined. Under a law called the Espionage Act of 1917, sharing information that could threaten national security is illegal. Obama used the law for the first time to go after government officials who shared classified, or secret, government information with the media that he said put the nation's security at risk.

U.S. president Donald J. Trump, who took office in 2017, has called much of the news media "the enemy of the people" when they report negative stories about him. Supporters at his public meetings have threatened and insulted members of the press covering these events. Some news outlets hire security guards to protect their reporters.

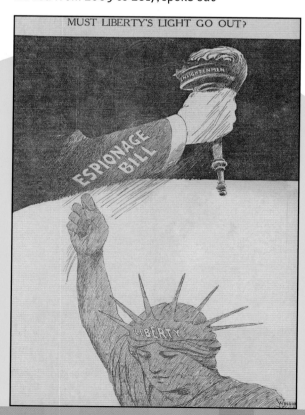

MUST LIBERTY'S LIGHT GO OUT?

ENLIGHTENMENT

ESPIONAGE BILL

LIBERTY

This editorial cartoon was published one month before the U.S. Congress passed the Espionage Act of 1917, which some thought would limit American's freedom.

ANAS AREMEYAW ANAS
Master of Disguise
(1978–)

Journalist Anas Aremeyaw Anas is world famous, but few people know what he looks like. How is that possible? Anas operates undercover, sometimes dressing up in crazy costumes, to expose crooks and corrupt leaders and businesses. Even when Anas speaks to large audiences, he has been known to wear a mask on stage to keep his appearance top secret.

In the United States, most news outlets have a policy against going undercover, except in extreme circumstances when there is no other way to tell an important story. In fact, most news organizations require their journalists to immediately identify themselves as reporters when asked. But Anas lives in the African country of Ghana, where he co-owns the newspaper *The New Crusading Guide,* and has made a career out of storytelling through the art of disguise.

This crafty reporter once wore a paper bag on his head with two eyeholes cut out, so he would look like a giant rock. Hiding along the roadside at the border of two African countries, Ghana and Côte d'Ivoire, Anas spied on trucks smuggling cacao beans. In another investigation, Anas posed as an assembly-line worker at a cookie factory, where he used a hidden camera to film rats running around the factory and maggots in the cookie flour. Anas's stories helped put the smugglers in jail and shut down the factory.

HEY, THAT'S A HOAX!
WAR OF THE WORLDS

A terrifying story rang out over the radio airwaves on October 30, 1938. Announcer Orson Welles reported that aliens had invaded the United States, blasting lethal heat rays as weapons. Based on the book *The War of the Worlds* by H. G. Wells, the radio show was so realistic that the host reminded listeners that the story was made up three times during the 62-minute broadcast. But when the show was over, rumors started flying. Supposedly, the tale had caused mass panic all over the United States: Allegedly, citizens flooded into the streets to see the epic space battle in the sky, and a New Jersey hospital treated frightened people for shock. Over the next couple of days, the hoax made front-page news. The headline, "US Terrorized By Radio's 'Men From Mars,'" appeared in the *San Francisco Chronicle,* and similar stories were published in major newspapers across the country.

Studies and investigations later found that most of the rumors of mass panic were just that, rumors. But the legend that the "War of the Worlds" hoax tricked the entire nation lives on to this day. As it turns out, it was mostly the newspapers that were fooled, not the American citizens.

This illustration of Martian fighting machines appeared in the H. G. Wells novel *The War of the Worlds* in 1898—some 40 years before Orson Welles told the dramatic story on the radio.

Who GIVES US THE News?

The growing number of media outlets offer news programs that represent many different points of view.

A free press does not necessarily mean an unbiased—or unprejudiced—press. The United States is made up of people from many different backgrounds, but most newspapers and television stations have long been run by white people, and mostly by men. So they haven't always done a good job of covering issues that are important to women, immigrants, or people of color. As a result, many of these groups have founded their own newspapers, TV networks, and websites. Some share information with readers in their native languages, and many provide perspectives that are difficult to find in much of the media.

NEWS IN MANY Languages

Long before Benjamin Franklin signed the Declaration of Independence, he was a successful newspaper publisher in colonial America. He saw an opportunity to reach the German community—one of the largest immigrant groups in America at the time. In 1732, Franklin published a paper in German and was credited with founding the first foreign-language paper in the Colonies.

Franklin's German paper failed, closing within two months, but other publishers succeeded many years later. By the 1800s, more than a thousand German newspapers sprang up in the United States. And in 1808, a group of wealthy Spanish immigrants in New Orleans, Louisiana, launched the United State's first Spanish-language newspaper, *El Misisipí*. The *Cherokee Phoenix* became the first Native American newspaper in 1828 and was printed in both English and the Cherokee language. The Cherokee Nation published it as a tool for fighting back against the U.S. government's drive to remove the Cherokee from their native land.

As more immigrants flooded into the United States during the 1800s, hundreds of new foreign-language papers popped up. Many faded quickly, but some are still around today.

Now a quarter of Americans get their news from multicultural media. Foreign-language publications in the United States reach many immigrant groups, including Chinese, Vietnamese, Pakistani, and Latin American communities, among many others. These outlets include huge media companies, like the Spanish-language TV network Univision and the Chinese-language newspapers *World Journal* and *Sing Tao Daily*. Some

Jorge Ramos reports the news. Ramos spent nearly five decades at Telemundo 47, a Spanish-language station in New York City.

major newspapers, such as Florida's *Miami Herald*, have Spanish-language editions. Tiny independent newspapers, blogs, and social media sites are also popular.

THE Changing FACE OF NEWS

News organizations are slowly becoming more diverse, with more people of color appearing on camera and working behind the scenes.

Today, mainstream newsrooms strive to be more diverse. Far more women are in journalism now than there used to be, and the mainstream news media are making an effort to hire reporters who are African American, Hispanic, and Asian as well as other minorities, so that all voices are heard. But people of color are still not equally represented in newsrooms, and that can affect the way news is covered.

One study found that local TV news in the United States is more likely to show pictures of criminals when they are African American, even though a majority of criminals are white. Another study found that TV network news in the United States shows more images of black people in stories about poverty despite the fact that the majority of people living in poverty in the United States are white. Other researchers found that as a result of this type of coverage, viewers were more likely to believe the falsehood that most black people are poor or that most criminals are black. Additional studies have found that TV news disproportionately depicts more Latinos as undocumented immigrants and Muslims as terrorists, even though most Latinos in the United States were born in the country and the vast majority of Muslims are law-abiding people. Although some progress has been made, the media still have work to do to make sure that all people are represented fairly and equally. So when you watch or read news, it's important to think about who is delivering it and how that might affect the way a story is presented.

AFRICAN-AMERICAN NEWSPAPERS MADE History

Today, some 200 U.S. newspapers specifically serve African-American audiences. These publications have a long history of speaking out against racism and slavery—beginning with the very first black-owned newspaper, founded in 1827. They have covered stories that the mainstream press has often overlooked, and their reporting has changed history. During World War I, the *Chicago Defender* wrote in favor of southern blacks moving north, where they could enjoy more freedoms. Their stories inspired many southern blacks to head north during the early 20th century, in what became known as the Great Migration. The *Defender* also reported on the civil rights movement of the 1950s and '60s, in which African Americans protested for equal rights, before most mainstream papers even started covering the topic.

Editors for another influential black paper called the *Pittsburgh Courier* wrote passionately about the need for major league baseball to allow African Americans into the league. Their campaign played a huge role in Jackie Robinson becoming the first black player in the major leagues in 1947.

THE FIRST AFRICAN-AMERICAN Newspaper

"WE WISH TO PLEAD OUR OWN CAUSE. TOO LONG HAVE OTHERS SPOKEN FOR US ..." These words were written in the first edition of *Freedom's Journal*, the first newspaper owned and operated by African Americans. First published in 1827, long before the end of slavery in the United States, the paper was founded in New York City by free African Americans Samuel Cornish and John B. Russwurm—the country's third African American to graduate from college. Many white-owned newspapers supported slavery or were extremely prejudiced against African Americans. But *Freedom's Journal* spoke out against slavery and discrimination and helped bring the African-American community together across different states and towns.

At its most popular, *Freedom's Journal* was distributed in 11 states, the District of Columbia, Europe, Canada, and on the Caribbean island of Haiti. The weekly newspaper only survived two years. By the start of the U.S. Civil War, some 40 African American–owned newspapers were in print throughout the United States.

Freedom's Journal, June 22, 1827

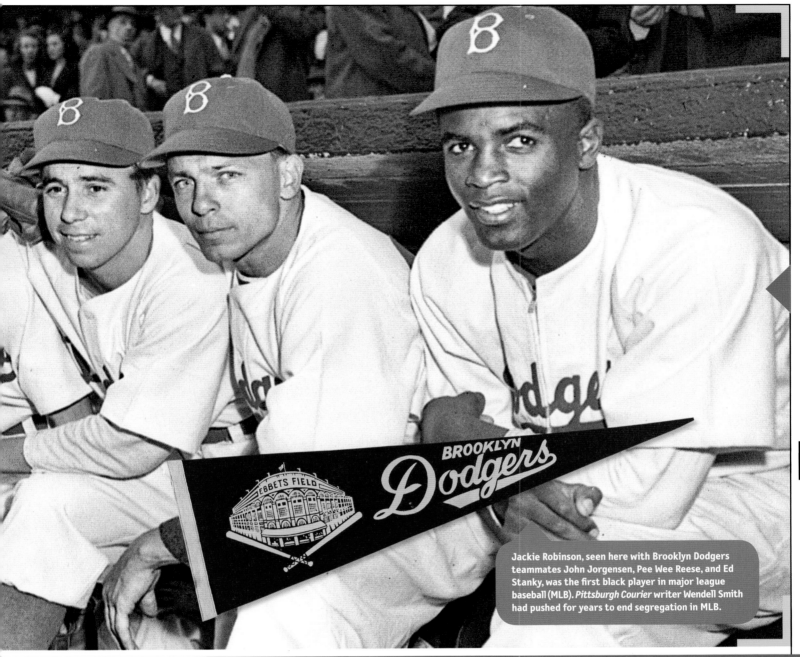

Jackie Robinson, seen here with Brooklyn Dodgers teammates John Jorgensen, Pee Wee Reese, and Ed Stanky, was the first black player in major league baseball (MLB). *Pittsburgh Courier* writer Wendell Smith had pushed for years to end segregation in MLB.

IDA B. WELLS

A Woman With a Powerful Pen
(1862–1931)

Born into slavery three years before the U.S. Civil War ended—Ida B. Wells became one of the most famous black women of her time. Wells began fighting injustice after a train conductor insisted that she give up her first-class seat to move to the "colored car," where black people were supposed to sit. When she refused, the conductor and other passengers tried to force her off the train. Wells sued the railroad company but eventually lost her case. So she took her fight to the African-American newspapers. Writing under the pen name "Iola," Wells spoke out against segregation laws. She later bought a share of a black-owned newspaper called the *Memphis Free Speech and Headlight*. After a close friend of Wells was accused of a crime and killed by a white mob, she became suspicious of the reasons given for these types of assaults. Wells conducted an in-depth investigation and discovered that, in most cases, the African-American victims had not committed the crimes for which they were accused. She found that these victims were attacked because they had dared to challenge white authority. After Wells printed her findings in 1892, an angry white mob destroyed her presses and ran her out of the South. She eventually settled in Chicago, where she continued her fight for the rights of African Americans and women.

Suffragists march through London, England, at the beginning of the 20th century, demanding that women get the right to vote.

A **VOICE** FOR **WOMEN**

In the 1800s, women's fight for equality in the workplace and women's suffrage, the right to vote, gained momentum in the United States. But women were rarely allowed to work at male-run newspapers, and the men were not paying much attention to women's issues. So women started publishing their own newspapers. In 1849, Amelia Bloomer, along with women's rights leader Elizabeth Cady Stanton, founded *The Lily*. In 1868, Stanton started *The Revolution* with famous suffragist Susan B. Anthony. The paper's motto was, "Men, their rights and nothing more; women, their rights and nothing less." These papers, and many that followed, helped organize the women's movement throughout the 1900s. For many women and minorities, writing about their causes meant risking their lives and their businesses. The publishers of many African-American, female-run, and other multicultural newspapers faced violent mobs who destroyed their presses, harassed and attacked them, or even ran them out of town.

Women's rights leaders Elizabeth Cady Stanton (left) and Susan B. Anthony in the late 1800s.

CONNIE CHUNG
Beloved Anchorperson (1946–)

Award-winning journalist Connie Chung broke boundaries in 1993 when she became the co-anchor of the *CBS Evening News*. A Chinese American, Chung was the first Asian and the second woman (after Barbara Walters) to anchor a major U.S. news program. When Chung first broke into journalism in the 1970s, TV news was a man's world with few people of color, but the networks were trying to become more inclusive and quickly spotted Chung's talent.

Chung worked her way up from local news reporter to the anchor desk, becoming one of the most beloved TV journalists of the time. Over the course of her career, Chung received an Emmy and a Peabody, two of the most prestigious awards in TV news, and worked for CBS, ABC, NBC, and CNN. In 1989, she launched her own TV show, called *Face to Face With Connie Chung*, which featured politics and celebrity news, and later went on to host *20/20*, one of the most popular news programs of the 1990s. Her career opened doors for many women and Asian Americans in the news business.

NATALIE MORALES
Multicultural Media Star (1972–)

An anchor and former host of the *Today Show*, Morales has been a correspondent for *Dateline NBC* and *NBC Nightly News*, and an anchor for MSNBC. With a Brazilian mother and a Puerto Rican father, Morales is trilingual—she can speak Portuguese, Spanish, and English fluently. Her father was in the U.S. Air Force, so she lived all over the world as a child, including Panama, Brazil, Spain, and the United States. And she has used her language skills to help her report on everything from local news stories in New York City to gripping international stories.

In October 2010, the story of 33 Chilean miners trapped underground for 69 days captivated the world. Morales was able to use her language skills to live-translate and report on the rescue as it happened. She has also covered breaking news stories such as wildfires in California, hurricanes, presidential elections, and the Olympic Games.

GLORIA STEINEM
A Voice for Women's Rights (1934–)

An outspoken advocate for women's equality, Gloria Steinem became one of the founding writers of *New York* magazine, where she made a name for herself writing about politics and women's issues. She then created a publication devoted completely to the women's movement. In 1971, she co-founded *Ms.* magazine, the first magazine created, owned, and operated entirely by women. *Ms.* was an instant success, selling out its first issue in eight days, and it is still publishing today.

ON THE EDGE

56

" **I**t's not like I'm actively looking for danger. I want to show people the wonders of nature," says *National Geographic* photographer Carsten Peter. He snapped this dramatic shot of scientists on Mount Etna, in Sicily, Italy, during a 2002 volcanic eruption that was big enough to be seen from space.

Peter's daring photographs of volcanoes, tornadoes, and ice caves have given people around the world a rare opportunity to get a close-up view of the powerful forces of nature.

Even with his professional training and so much preparation, getting these intimate shots is risky. So what's it like to stand on the edge of an exploding volcano? "This lava lake is bubbling above you, and if the wall breaks ... you know you do not have a chance at all," says Peter. "Often the people scream behind me, 'We have to move, we have to move,' but I'm so focused [on] my camera. I'm just lost [in the] moment." The result? Photos, like this one, that capture that split second when nature is both terrifying and spectacular.

NHIỆT LIỆT CHÀO MỪNG KỶ NIỆM 78 NĂM
NGÀY THÀNH LẬP ĐẢNG CỘNG SẢN VIỆT NAM
3/2 (1930-2008)

This billboard in Vietnam features government propaganda celebrating the anniversary of the founding of the Vietnamese Communist Party.

3

PROPAGANDA, Half-Truths, and HOAXES

Propaganda is an organized campaign that spreads information through the media, but it is the opposite of news. The purpose of news is to provide accurate information and facts about what is happening in the world. News strives for balance, meaning that it does not promote one cause over another and includes different perspectives. The goal of news is to inform the public. Propaganda, however, aims to change people's ideas and actions and supports only one point of view.

HOW TO SPOT
Propaganda

Because it's easy to confuse propaganda with news, it's important to know how to spot it when you see it.

Some kinds of propaganda can be quite harmful. They can intentionally mislead people by twisting facts or spreading rumors and lies—such as when politicians spread false stories about other candidates or when large companies spread incorrect information to help sell their products. But propaganda isn't always negative. It can also be used to stir up support for a cause—for example, recruiting soldiers to sign up for the military—or to spread public safety messages.

Propaganda exists everywhere—on the internet, social media, radio, and TV, as well as in newspapers and movies, and any other place that information is shared with the public.

Up to 100,000 people perform during North Korea's Mass Games, a propaganda event designed to show unity among the country's citizens.

"The Albanians" artwork on the National Historic Museum in Tirana, Albania, tells how centuries of Albanians have fought against invasions and occupation in their country. It was designed as propaganda for the country's socialist political party.

CAUSE FOR **Confusion**

Propaganda can also hide the truth by creating confusion. For example, if a negative news story comes out about a public figure, that person might go to the media and offer several different, false explanations for what happened. The goal is to confuse the public about what is true and cast doubt on whether the original story was correct.

In one example from 2018, a former Russian agent was poisoned while living in England. When the British accused Russia of the attack, Russia denied any involvement. Russian officials also offered all the following explanations for why Britain would want to accuse them: to make Russia look bad, to spoil the upcoming World Cup soccer match, and to distract from a political crisis in Britain. They also suggested that other countries were responsible for this killing.

Russia delivered these confusing messages through various media outlets, attempting to make the public question Britain's accusations. In September 2018, the British government charged two Russian agents with the poisoning. The evidence was so strong that the United States issued financial penalties against Russia as punishment. Despite Russia's tireless propaganda campaign, Britain's original accusations turned out to be true.

May points the finger at Russia over 'reckless' poisoning of spy

Anushka Asthana
Andrew Roth
Luke Harding

the incident an "indiscriminate and reckless act", she said Boris Johnson had summoned Russia's ambassador to Whitehall and demanded an

The story of a poisoned spy made headlines around the world in 2018. In this article, then British prime minister Theresa May accuses Russia of the crime.

IN *WWI,* BRITAIN *CUT* THE *UNDERSEA CABLES* THAT ALLOWED GERMANY TO DISTRIBUTE *PROPAGANDA* OUTSIDE ITS BORDERS.

THE **Blame** GAME

Another common propaganda technique, called scapegoating, involves blaming other people or groups of people—often different cultural groups—for problems, sometimes giving them mean nicknames or making them seem cruel or scary. Scapegoating usually targets groups who are relatively powerless and cannot fight back with the same resources as their accusers.

Throughout history and around the world, immigrants and people of color have been frequent targets of scapegoating, with politicians and citizens often blaming them for everything from economic problems to the spread of disease. After the U.S. Civil War, African Americans newly freed from slavery were frequent scapegoats, often accused of crimes they did not commit.

Scapegoating continues today. Like in many other countries, some American politicians try to blame crime on undocumented immigrants who are in the country illegally, even though studies show that Americans are more likely to commit crimes than immigrants. But this propaganda—spread through political advertisements, campaign rallies, and TV appearances—is often successful because it plays to people's emotions, rather than relying on facts.

A man shows support for a proposed border wall between the United States and Mexico at a rally in Johnson City, Tennessee, U.S.A., in 2018.

HOW DOES IT WORK?

The more people hear a message, the more they believe it. What's surprising is that even the false messages stick. Studies have shown that even when we know information is incorrect, we often later remember it as true. This can affect people's ideas and the decisions they make, such as who to vote for or what causes they support. The power of propaganda has helped elect politicians, played a major role in winning wars, and changed public opinion about major issues. It's important to be able to spot propaganda, so you aren't fooled by information slanted toward one opinion. That way, you can decide for yourself what you believe.

? Have you heard a celebrity or politician tell a story and found out later that it wasn't true?

These protesters gathered in London, England, in 2016 to accuse the U.K. government of racism and scapegoating Muslims.

THE Recipe FOR PROPAGANDA

Political candidates, corporations, individuals, and groups who support certain causes can launch propaganda campaigns. But regardless of who is behind these efforts, effective campaigns often have many of the same ingredients:

1 Play to emotions—Tap into people's hope, fear, anger, or sympathy, rather than relying on facts.

2 Stick to simple messages—Use catchy words, slogans, phrases, and visual symbols that stick in people's heads and are easy for the public to remember.

3 Repeat, repeat, repeat—When people see the same words, pictures, or ideas over and over again, they are more likely to believe them.

4 Know the audience—Propaganda campaigns often target people who will be most receptive to their messages, including specific communities, age groups, or those who come from certain cultural backgrounds or hold certain beliefs.

5 Use peer pressure—Propaganda may try to convince you that everyone else supports a certain idea, so you should, too.

6 Get celebrity endorsements—When famous people promote an idea, their support can go a long way toward swaying public opinion.

Daddy, what did YOU do in the Great War?

"Daddy, what did YOU do in the Great War?" reads this well-known poster from World War I. It played to emotions as it tried to convince young men to volunteer for the military.

★REAGAN

FOR PRESIDENT
Let's make America great again.

Presidential candidates use a variety of propaganda materials to drum up support for their campaigns:
(PINS) TOP: Bill Clinton (D), 1992;
BOTTOM: Dwight D. "Ike" Eisenhower (R), 1952
(POSTER) Ronald Reagan (R), 1980
(SIGN) Barack Obama (D), 2008

CLINTON PRO-CHANGE GORE '92

I LIKE IKE

CHANGE WE CAN BELIEVE IN
BarackObama.com

THE Horrors OF PROPAGANDA

Although propaganda has existed throughout history, World War I (1914–18) was the first time governments launched organized campaigns to spread this type of information, even opening special offices in charge of propaganda. But in World War II (1939–1945), the German dictator Adolf Hitler took propaganda to a new level, using the power of the media to commit one of the most horrible tragedies in the history of the world—the murder of six million Jews, as well as hundreds of thousands of other people Hitler didn't like, such as other ethnic minorities and people with disabilities. It would take six years for the Allied powers, which included the United States, Britain, China, and the Soviet Union (now Russia and other countries), to stop Hitler's reign of terror.

What happens when leaders disseminate false information?

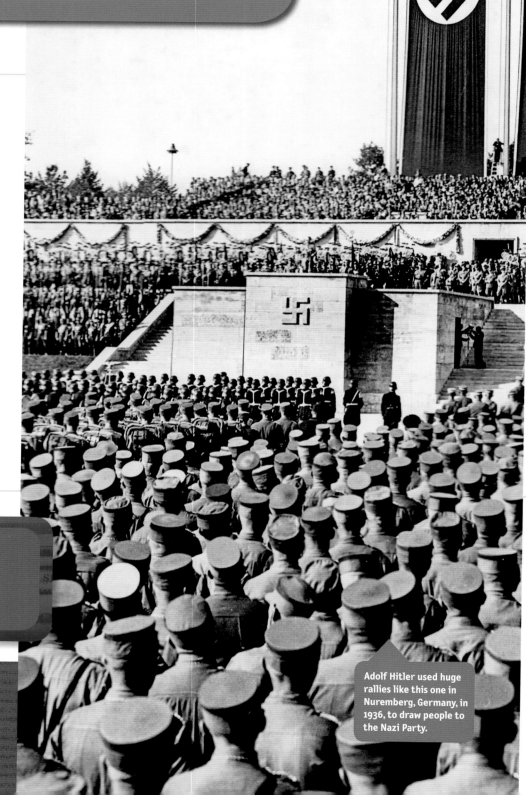

Adolf Hitler used huge rallies like this one in Nuremberg, Germany, in 1936, to draw people to the Nazi Party.

THE NAZI PROPAGANDA Machine

Through Hitler's Ministry of Public Enlightenment and Propaganda, his Nazi Party controlled all sources of information in Germany, including newspapers, radio, movies, museum exhibits, and textbooks. The Nazis burned thousands of library books that didn't support their ideas. Racist messages and pictures appeared in newspapers, on posters, literally everywhere. Nazi films made Hitler look like a hero while portraying Jewish people as less than human. Anti-Semitic (anti-Jewish) messages were even included in children's books.

The Nazis also recognized that images have power. The swastika—a cross with the ends bent at right angles—became the symbol of the Nazi Party, appearing on flags, soldiers' armbands, posters, badges, and more. To this day, a swastika stands for hate and anti-Semitism. The Nazis also created scary movies that tried to turn the German public against Jews.

To gain support for their terrible actions, the Nazis intentionally misled the public. In August 1939, they even staged a fake Polish attack on a German radio station to gain public support for an invasion of Poland.

Controlling all media allowed the Nazi Party to spread lies as well as hatred and fear of Jewish people, blaming them for the country's loss in World War I and for Germany's economic problems. Having convinced many people of these lies, the Nazis won much of the German public's support and frightened many others into keeping quiet. Two out of every three Jewish people in Europe had been killed by the time the Nazis were defeated. The Nazis' tight control of the media made it possible for them to hide these killings.

This car carried a Nazi message throughout Vienna, Austria, prior to a 1924 election.

HEY, THAT'S A HOAX! PAPER TRAIL

In 1983, a German magazine called *Stern* claimed to have obtained secret diaries written by Nazi leader Adolf Hitler. The magazine printed the first in what was supposed to have been a series of articles based on the documents. The *Sunday Times* of London also agreed to pay *Stern* £250,000 for the rights to the diaries. But before the *Times* went to press, German experts examined the diaries and found that they were made of paper created after World War II. Since Hitler died in April 1945, there was no way these journals could have belonged to him. *Stern* and the *Times* were horrified to learn that the diaries were a hoax, and immediately ceased publication of the articles.

RUSSIAN **Propaganda** IN THE 2016 U.S. ELECTION

Less violent, but still harmful, campaigns of disinformation are common today. Social media makes it easier than ever to spread false messages. This was especially true during the U.S. presidential race of 2016, between Hillary Clinton and Donald Trump. In election years, propaganda supporting and opposing different candidates is to be expected, but it normally comes from groups inside the country. In 2016, however, a storm of propaganda came from Russia. It's against U.S. law for foreign countries to try to influence U.S. elections, so this was an illegal and secretive campaign. The campaign spread its materials—such as political messages and false information about how to vote—as if it was coming from Americans. But actually, it was being created in Russia and distributed through fake social media accounts in the United States.

In 2018, the U.S. Department of Justice charged 13 Russians with trying to disrupt the American elections. The Justice Department and U.S. intelligence agencies found that these Russians had hired hundreds of people to set up the phony social media accounts, organize political rallies, and pay for political ads on social media.

Facebook found that at least 80,000 posts came from 120 fake Facebook pages run by Russians. The posts were received by some 29 million Americans and were likely shared with millions more. At least 18 YouTube accounts were linked to Russian propaganda campaigns. And Twitter announced that a Russian group had set up some 3,840 false accounts, producing millions of tweets. As this book goes to press, all of these investigations are ongoing.

This isn't happening only in the United States. Russian-backed groups have tried to interfere in elections around the world. The United States, other countries, and social media companies are now on high alert, keeping a lookout for fake accounts by foreign governments. But there's a lot of work still to do, and identifying these fake accounts is difficult. That's why it's important for social media users to make sure they know where information comes from (see chapter 5), so they aren't tricked.

Presidential candidates Donald Trump and Hillary Clinton face off in a 2016 debate in Las Vegas, Nevada.

FAKE FACEBOOK POSTS CREATED BY **RUSSIANS** WERE RECEIVED BY SOME *29 MILLION* **AMERICANS** LEADING UP TO THE **2016 ELECTION.**

Slanted SCIENCE

Individuals aren't the only targets of propaganda. Science can come under fire as well. How is that possible? Well, sometimes science reveals information that conflicts with people's beliefs. For example, a lot of information on social media claims that the measles vaccine causes autism. Science has proven this to be wrong, but the false messages make some parents afraid to vaccinate their children, leading to outbreaks of the dangerous disease.

Science also can reveal facts that threaten moneymaking businesses, such as that tobacco use is unhealthy and that fossil fuels—including coal, oil, and natural gas—cause climate change. For years, the tobacco and fossil fuel industries have fought back against these scientific findings, launching campaigns of false and confusing information to try to turn the truth upside down.

TOP: A protester at a 2019 rally in New York City opposes a vaccine law proposed by state lawmakers. FAR LEFT: As a result of false information, some people have refused to give their children measles vaccines. NEAR LEFT: A medical facility in Vancouver, Washington State, U.S.A., posted this sign during a measles outbreak among unvaccinated people.

1 Single-dose 0.5-mL Via
MEASLES, MUMPS, AND
RUBELLA VIRUS VACCIN
M-M-R® II

HEALTH ALERT

Patient and visitor safety is our top priority.

Due to the rising number of confirmed measles cases in Clark County, guests under the age of 12 and those that are not vaccinated or are immunocompromised are respectfully asked to leave the facility immediately.

Thank you for your understanding.

PeaceHealth
Southwest Medical Center

Many factories, in addition to other human activity, contribute to global warming. Scientists have proven this to be true, but still some people claim that climate change is a hoax.

SMOKE Screen

One of the longest and most hard-fought battles over science took place between public health officials and the tobacco industry. Today, everyone knows that smoking is bad for you. But tobacco companies have denied this for years.

As far back as the 1940s, a number of scientific studies found that smoking causes lung cancer and other health problems. In 1964, the U.S. government put out a report with the same findings. Over the following 30 years, the tobacco industry fought all efforts to limit the use of tobacco products. And one of their most effective strategies was to question these studies.

The tobacco industry formed its own group, called the Tobacco Industry Research Committee (later called the Council for Tobacco Research), which produced research challenging the idea that smoking kills people. Despite thousands of studies showing that smoking is harmful to people's health, the tobacco industry studies managed to confuse the debate.

Eventually, a combination of public education about the dangers of smoking and lawsuits against the tobacco industry changed everything. Today, it's illegal to smoke in most restaurants and offices in the United States, and there are far fewer smokers now than 30 years ago. And, most important, the majority of Americans now know that smoking is bad for them and support laws that reduce tobacco use.

Now a new controversy is brewing over vaping—or using e-cigarettes to inhale vapor that contains nicotine, an addictive substance also found in regular cigarettes. Vaping devices do not use tobacco, which is found in regular cigarettes and has been linked to many health problems. But that does not mean that vaping is safe.

The propaganda battle is already in full gear. Researchers and organizations who question the safety of vaping are attacked on social media. The attacks confuse the public, making people uncertain about who to trust. In the meantime, more and more young people are starting to vape, in part because the propaganda makes them think it is safe. As this book goes to press, thousands of cases of a mysterious vaping-related lung disease have been reported— mostly in young adults—including 47 deaths in the United States alone, according the Centers for Disease Control and Prevention.

E-cigarettes used for vaping can be harmful to your health. E-cigarette companies use propaganda to try to convince you otherwise.

I miss my lung, Bob.

California Department Of Health Services. Funded By The Tobacco Tax Initiative.

© 1998 California Department of Health Services

This anti-smoking ad from 2000 reminded people that smoking causes lung cancer. It played on a popular cigarette advertising campaign that tried to make smoking look adventurous.

CLIMATE CHANGE
Heats Up

For years, another fierce debate has taken place over climate change. The science is clear: Earth's climate is warming, and these changes are harmful to the environment. The science points to greenhouse gas emissions from burning fossil fuels as the main cause of the warming. The problem is, fossil fuels are the world's biggest sources of energy. And switching to eco-friendly energy, such as wind and solar power, could mean less business for companies that produce fossil fuels.

Many oil companies have now started to accept that climate change is real and have proposed some measures to curb it. But that's a recent change after a long battle for public opinion. For years, fossil fuel companies funded misleading studies that showed the climate isn't really warming that much or that the problem is not caused by humans. These false findings are still repeated over and over and have been so effective that some lawmakers and citizens now believe that climate change either isn't real or is not caused by humans. This has slowed efforts to combat climate change. And the debate shows no signs of ending.

Climate change causes temperatures to rise and sea ice to melt, threatening polar bear survival in the Arctic.

? What does the news you read or watch say about climate change?

How to Spot Shifty Science

Most scientists conduct responsible research. They try to answer important questions about health, technology, space, the environment, and many other topics. But some bad studies slip through the cracks and get more attention from the media than they deserve. So how can you spot the false information? It can be difficult, and even journalists can struggle to tell the difference. The most important question to ask is: Who is funding the study? Is an organization or company behind it that may want to sway public opinion in its own favor? If a candy company is behind a study that claims "eating candy will make you healthier," think twice before believing that research. And in general, if the results of a study sound too good to be true, they probably are!

On September 8, 2019, Hurricane Dorian slammed into the Bahamas and then pounded the islands for two days. Scientists expect warmer temperatures and higher sea levels to lead to more strong hurricanes.

THE POWER OF Images

This World War I poster—designed to encourage young men to join the U.S. Army—is one of the most memorable images in American history.

In propaganda campaigns, images can be as important as words, sometimes more so. These images are called visual propaganda, and they can include anything from symbols, such as flags or logos, to special colors, posters, videos, photographs, GIFs, and other images you might find on the internet.

These images make ideas easier to remember. A study found that people can remember far more pictures than words—as many as 2,000 images at a time with almost complete accuracy. And they are more likely to remember a message if it is paired with an image. So including pictures gives propaganda an extra punch.

I WANT YOU

for the U.S. ARMY ENLIST NOW

JAMES MONTGOMERY FLAGG

Get behind
the Girl he left behind him

Join the
land army

During World War I, fundraising posters convinced more than 15,000 volunteers to join the Woman's Land Army of America—in which women worked on farms to support the needs of the country.

Patriotic POSTERS

During World War I, television didn't exist yet and radio was not widely available, so printed posters were one of the most effective ways to communicate with the public. In the U.K. and the United States, many war posters encouraged men to join the military. One of the most famous U.S. propaganda posters of all time featured Uncle Sam saying, "I want you for the U.S. Army."

And because food was in short supply in Europe, some posters encouraged women at home to eat corn instead of wheat and to grow vegetables in "victory gardens," so there would be more food to send to troops overseas. One poster read, "The kitchen is the key to victory. Eat less bread."

Propaganda efforts kicked into high gear again for World War II. The United States alone produced some 200,000 posters over the course of the war, including one that is still famous to this day. Most men were away at war in Europe, so the government

The famous Rosie the Riveter ad campaign was introduced during World War II to encourage women to join the workforce, where they took on the positions for men who were away at war.

needed women—who mostly stayed home in those days—to go to work to keep the war effort going. In a poster that remains a symbol of pride for working women, "Rosie the Riveter" flexes her muscle under the words "We Can Do It!"

75

POSITIVE
Propaganda

Some propaganda tries to change people's behavior to make them healthier and safer. Today, most kids know not to get into cars with strangers, and almost everyone wears a seat belt. This is because of public education campaigns about safety and health.

A public education campaign that began in 1979 and continues today features the character McGruff the Crime Dog. For years, McGruff urged people to "take a bite out of crime" by locking their doors and giving kids safety tips for dealing with strangers. Today, McGruff helps teach kids about the dangers of cyberbullying.

And you may have seen the "Click It or Ticket" message on billboards as you ride down the highway in the United States. That's also a public service campaign, designed to remind people that wearing a seat belt is a law. Partially as a result of public education efforts like these, 90 percent of people in the United States were wearing seat belts by 2016.

COMICS AND **Movies**

During World War II, the U.S. government asked Hollywood and comic book publishers to create anti-Nazi and pro-war story lines. In fact, that's how the comic book character Captain America was created in 1941. The comic book's first cover shows the Cap punching Hitler in the face.

Throughout the war, Hollywood movies depicted American heroes fighting Nazis and Japanese villains. Some of these movies also used racist stereotypes to turn U.S. citizens against the Japanese, who sided with Germany in the war. And during the Cold War (1945–1991) between the United States and the Soviet Union (now Russia and other countries), secret agent James Bond tried to outwit Soviet spies. Today, modern movie heroes sometimes battle terrorists.

These stories can unfairly promote stereotypes about people from certain countries or cultures. It's important to keep any eye out for these negative messages so you don't let these fictional stories affect your real-life opinions.

? Have you seen a movie or TV show in which someone from a foreign country was the bad guy?

THEODOR GEISEL
Dr. Seuss Marches to War
(1904–1991)

Theodor Geisel—the author and illustrator of the classic Dr. Seuss children's books—was having a hard time concentrating on Horton the Elephant. It was June 1940, and World War II was raging in Europe. Geisel believed with all his heart that the United States needed to get involved in the war to help beat the Nazis and their allies at the time, fascist Italy and imperial Japan. So he turned his attention (and his pen) toward the war effort.

From 1941 to 1942, Geisel drew some 400 political cartoons for a New York newspaper called *PM*. Many of the cartoons showed unkind, uncomplimentary stereotypes of Japanese people—who were considered U.S. enemies during the war. Typical of the time, these cartoons ended up promoting racist ideas about the Japanese.

In 1943, Geisel joined the U.S. Army and was assigned to work with movie studios in Hollywood to create propaganda supporting the U.S. war effort. Among other characters, he invented a series of animated movies about a bumbling character who showed troops what NOT to do, and battled against Nazi leader Adolf Hitler, who was portrayed as the devil.

After the war, Geisel returned to creating children's books. He wrote and illustrated more than 60 books during his lifetime. In the 1970s, he expressed regret about his early drawings that promoted stereotypes about people of color. But some of Seuss's books remain controversial today.

This comic by Geisel in 1942 encourages Americans to face the hard truth of war and the need to help the Allied forces.

famous FLUB

OPRAH'S UNWANTED MAKEOVER
When famous talk show host Oprah Winfrey lost 67 pounds in 1989, *TV Guide* ran a picture of her on its cover revealing her glamorous new look. Except the picture was a phony. Oprah's head was placed on the body of a well-known singer and actress at the time, Ann-Margret—without the permission of either woman. The truth came out when Ann-Margret's fashion designer recognized the dress in the picture. *TV Guide* admitted that running the image was an error in judgment. As for Oprah, she declined to comment on the matter, but her spokesperson said Oprah would never pose on top of a pile of money or wear that kind of dress.

POLITICAL CARTOONS

Comic books like *Captain America* can tell simple, lighthearted stories, but some cartoonists take things a step further, offering a creative and thoughtful take on politics. These political cartoons, which use humor to express opinions about the news, can be an effective form of propaganda.

The first political cartoons popped up in England in the mid-1700s. The trend quickly spread to the British Colonies in America, where cartoons were printed in newspapers and displayed in taverns and coffeehouses—a surefire way to draw in the crowds.

Benjamin Franklin created the first political cartoon in the American Colonies. Published in 1754, his now famous drawing showed the colonies as a snake divided into pieces, with each colony as a separate section. The cartoon became a symbol of the American Revolution, calling on the Colonies to join together in the fight against England.

These clever and sometimes funny images went a long way in attracting readers. By 1900, some 500 political cartoonists worked at American newspapers, and they have been a staple of newspapers and magazines ever since. Today, websites publish more political cartoons than newspapers do, and their readers share these images widely online.

James Gillray's "The Plumb-Pudding in Danger," 1805

JAMES GILLRAY
Illustration Influencer
(1756–1815)

As one of the first political cartoonists, James Gillray often made England's King George III—whom Gillray nicknamed "Farmer George"—the butt of his jokes. French military leader Napoleon Bonaparte was another favorite target. Gillray's cartoons were beloved by the public and feared by the powerful, as Gillray was fond of making royalty and world leaders look like fools.

He created nearly 1,000 prints, but in 1805, he penned what many consider to be the greatest political cartoon of all time. In "The Plumb-Pudding in Danger," British statesman William Pitt and Napoleon sit at a dinner table, each carving out their piece of the globe, pictured as a traditional British dessert called plum pudding. At the time, Pitt and Napoleon were in a battle for world power. This cheeky cartoon showed how crazy it was that the two men thought they could have the whole world to themselves.

This illustration by Benjamin Franklin was the first political cartoon printed in the American Colonies.

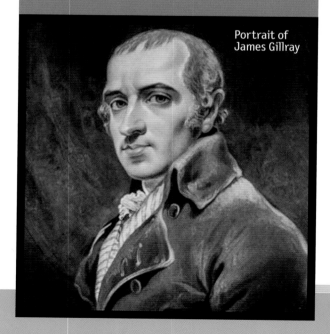

Portrait of James Gillray

TOP: The comic strip "Doonesbury" is known for its political commentary. This strip, from 2019, points out how important local news is for communities. **LEFT:** Anonymous or unnamed sources can be the key to unlocking a big story, but they can also be misused or overused in reporting. This 2019 cartoon published in the *New Yorker* pokes fun at this issue. **BELOW:** Editorial cartoons often question political decisions that impact national security around the world.

"He's Anonymous and I'm Unnamed Source."

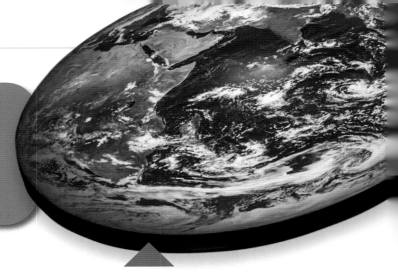

HOAXES AND Conspiracy THEORIES

Propaganda can also take the form of an elaborate hoax, when someone tricks people into believing something that isn't true. And social media has made it easier than ever for these false stories to spread. Experts say social media posts that generate strong emotions or include bizarre stories are among the most common to "go viral." So hoaxes can spread across the internet like wildfire. Sometimes these hoaxes go beyond being just a big trick and become a conspiracy theory— a made-up story claiming that powerful people are secretly behind an event or crime they are trying to cover up. Not all hoaxes are harmful, but it's important for people to be responsible with what they share, because some false stories can have serious consequences.

IT'S A Conspiracy!

Sometimes a hoax can turn into a conspiracy theory and have extremely dangerous consequences. In 2016, a false rumor spread on social media saying that a pizza restaurant in Washington, D.C., was linked to a major political party and that a

This image of Earth is altered to make it look flat. Fake images like these can feed false conspiracy theories that Earth is flat instead of round.

well-known political candidate and her campaign manager had turned the restaurant into a hub for illegal activity involving children. The restaurant started receiving threatening phone calls and messages. One afternoon, a man armed with a gun—who believed the conspiracy theory was true— showed up to "investigate" and fired shots inside the restaurant. Fortunately, no one was hurt, and the man was arrested.

HEY, THAT'S A HOAX! THE GREAT MOON PRANK

Not all hoaxes are propaganda. Some are just hilarious! In 1835, the *New York Sun* newspaper ran a six-part series claiming that a famous scientist had discovered life on the moon. As the story goes, the scientist peered at the moon through one of the world's most powerful telescopes. He spotted humanlike figures with bat wings, beavers that walked on two feet, and unicorns with blue beards. He also saw rivers, lush plant life, and beautiful crystals. At a time when people knew almost nothing about outer space, readers totally believed the story. The *Sun* only came clean when a competing newspaper revealed the hoax.

A VIEW OF
THE INHABITANTS OF THE MOON,
AS SEEN THROUGH THE TELESCOPE OF SIR JOHN HERSCHEL.

Not all conspiracy theories lead to violence. Sometimes they simply cause confusion or challenge those in charge. A small group of people believe the theory that Earth is actually flat—even though scientists have known for more than 2,000 years that Earth is round. Despite the airplanes and ships that frequently travel *around* the globe, these people use flawed reasoning to "prove" their theories. They believe that because Earth looks flat, it is flat. On social media and conspiracy websites, they claim that all photos of the round globe are doctored and that government agencies simply made up the idea that Earth is round. But these ideas are flat-out wrong.

Another "out there" conspiracy theory is that NASA faked all six moon landings by U.S. astronauts. In reality, some 400,000 scientists worked on the moon missions, 12 American astronauts have walked on the moon, and NASA brought back 842 pounds of space rock—and then

American astronaut David R. Scott salutes in this actual NASA photograph taken on the moon on August 1, 1971, during the Apollo 15 mission.

shared the rocks with scientists all over the world.

The flat Earth and moon landing conspiracy theories are based on faulty logic—that because the science behind these ideas can be hard to understand, it must not be true. These groups have spread so much propaganda online that they can actually make people question scientific fact.

"**Everyone** is entitled to his **own opinion,** but not his own set of **facts.**"

—U.S. SENATOR DANIEL PATRICK MOYNIHAN

Harmful HOAX

While some hoaxes, like the one about the pizza restaurant, can lead to violence, others can cause financial harm. One hoax in 2013 targeted a bank in Australia. Someone created a fake document with the logo of a major bank on it and sent it to the media. The document stated that the bank was planning to pull its funding from a major coal mining project. The hoax was so convincing that some news organizations published the information. As a result, the bank's stock value temporarily dropped by about $300 million. The story was quickly revealed as a hoax, but not before doing major damage.

WHY PEOPLE FALL FOR False INFORMATION

So what makes people believe propaganda and hoaxes so easily? We are more likely to trust information that confirms what we already think is true. For example, we will more easily believe positive information about a public figure we like and negative information about someone we don't like. That's why a lot of people fall for falsehoods on the internet—because the information strengthens what they already believe. At the same time, we often ignore information that doesn't support our beliefs—even if it's 100 percent correct.

PHOTOS THAT STRETCHED *THE TRUTH*

Hoaxes can be visual, too. Some are just harmless jokes, but others can be more serious, making people believe that an event actually happened. Some start out as a joke but can upset people, such as the photo of a shark swimming down a flooded street. Legitimate news organizations do not publish fake images; however, many irresponsible social media accounts and websites spread these doctored pictures.

Because of today's technology, false photos spread faster and farther than ever before. But believe it or not, photo fakery has been around for hundreds of years—long before computers and social media were even invented. These doctored photos from history and today show how photos have been tricking people for a very long time. (To learn how to spot a fake photo, see page 128.)

Wait, is that Abraham Lincoln (above left)? Or is it proslavery politician John C. Calhoun (above right), who represented South Carolina before the Civil War? Actually, it's both of them! After Lincoln died in 1865, someone altered this photo by putting Lincoln's head on Calhoun's body to make the former president look more heroic. The photo was not discovered to be a fake for another hundred years!

FALSE BATTLEGROUND

In this photo, U.S. Civil War commander and future U.S. president Ulysses S. Grant appears before his troops in City Point, Virginia, in 1864. Except, this scene never happened. It's three photos combined into one. And those aren't Grant's Union troops in the background. They are Confederate soldiers who were captured in a completely different part of Virginia. This image was created in 1902, some 40 years after the scene supposedly took place. And it wasn't until 2007 that historians realized the photo was doctored.

SCENE

HORSE

HEAD

BOGUS BLASTOFF

The North Korean government has a long history of faking photos to use as propaganda. Photo experts suspect that the appearance of the country's leader Kim Jong Un is often altered in photographs—especially the shape of his ears! But this photo shows an underwater missile launch that probably never happened. Aerospace experts said that some photos of the event showed a trail of white smoke, whereas others did not. Also, the reflection in the water is at the wrong angle. Apparently, this attempt to show military might was a major flop.

FISHY PHOTO

A shark washed ashore in a hurricane and now is swimming down the flooded city streets of Houston, Texas, U.S.A.! Some 87,000 people shared that story and photo, and 140,000 people "liked" it on Twitter. The story is a fake. But that didn't stop it from going viral, or spreading around the world on social media in a matter of minutes.

THE FACE OF COURAGE

84

In spring 1989, protesters took to the streets in Beijing, the capital of China, to demand more freedom and less corruption in the Communist country—where citizens have limited rights. The day before this photo was taken, the Chinese government had violently attacked many of the protesters.

On June 5—in a plaza called Tiananmen Square—this unarmed man had the courage to face off with a row of Chinese tanks. Eventually, soldiers physically moved him out of the way, but not before the scene was caught on camera.

This image traveled around the globe and appeared on the front page of newspapers all over the world. The unidentified man—known only as "Tank Man"—became an international hero for having the courage to stand up to a powerful, unjust government. To this day, the famous photo is known worldwide as the symbol of the Tiananmen Square protests.

With smartphones and tablets, people literally have news at their fingertips 24/7.

4

Media TODAY

Not so long ago, the primary way for people to share information with the public was through the journalists who worked for TV, radio, or newspapers. But the internet changed all this, creating a flood of information—some accurate and some not—from millions of different sources.

A cameraman and reporter conduct an interview in Auckland, New Zealand, in 2017.

WHAT IT MEANS TO BE A
Journalist

You don't have to watch sports news to find out about your favorite athletes or read gossip magazines to get the scoop on celebrities, because famous people can now talk directly to their fans on social media.

When Donald J. Trump became U.S. president in 2017, he was the first president to use Twitter—instead of traditional news organizations—as his primary way of communicating with the public, even using it to make big announcements and to speak out against people with whom he disagrees. But you don't have to be famous to spread information. Regular people can tweet or post videos showing anything from a local parade to a severe snowstorm in their town. With so many people spreading information, how can you tell the difference between reliable journalism and everything else?

It's the way journalists do their jobs that sets them apart from the pack. Professional journalists follow a code of ethics (see page 98) and have an organized system for researching stories and verifying facts. In the following pages, you'll see that journalists go to extraordinary lengths to get a story right. It's a journalist's job to confirm the facts, rely on solid sources, be fair and transparent, and avoid bias.

 Can something be considered news if it is only a few lines in a social media post?

88

Confirm THE FACTS

Journalists often say that the easiest way to get something wrong is to take someone at their word. That means they confirm everything someone tells them, no matter how obvious it seems. Instead of sharing the latest rumor trending online, reporters check the facts themselves.

Reliable journalists have an organized process of gathering information and verifying facts through research, interviews, and eyewitness accounts. And that's no small task. Reporting a story means working through three layers of information and understanding arguments on all sides of complicated issues. Firsthand information is the most accurate, because that's when you see an event with your own eyes—for example, you see a house fire on Cranberry Lane. A statement by an official with expert knowledge of the incident, such as the fire chief, is also considered the equivalent of firsthand information. Secondhand information is when you hear the story from someone else. For example, a

woman runs up to tell you she saw a fire on Cranberry Lane. Thirdhand information is the least reliable. That's when people say they heard about the fire but did not actually see it.

Secondhand or thirdhand information can provide a good lead on a story, but reporters keep interviewing people and researching until they get as close to firsthand information as possible. Even then, misinformation is still possible. The police could make a mistake and identify the wrong suspect in a crime, for instance, or the story can change as more information becomes available.

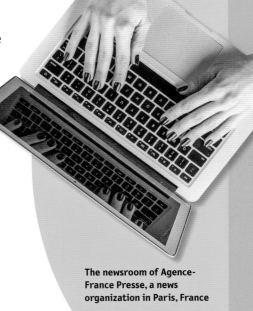

The newsroom of Agence-France Presse, a news organization in Paris, France

89

Question EVERYTHING

To get a story right, journalists ask a lot of questions. Are the time, date, and location of the events correct? If the information comes from social media, is the account real, or is it a false profile that someone has created? Has the information been checked directly with the people in the story—including name spellings and ages—and with others who would have direct knowledge of the subject?

Journalists verify information independently whenever possible. Among other questions, reporters must also consider if a story could put someone in physical danger or hurt someone's reputation, and if so, what are the compelling reasons to publish it.

BE Fair

Reliable news organizations strive to present fair and balanced stories. They try to be as objective as possible, which means they give all sides of an issue serious consideration in their stories. Going straight to the person at the center of a story is important, but that alone isn't enough. Reporters seek out different opinions and interview other people who may have seen an event, know the person in the story, or are directly involved in other ways.

To cover a parade, a reporter would interview people who ride on the floats, members of the crowd, and event organizers, who would all likely have positive things to say. But an interview with a neighbor who's angry about the trash left behind after the event tells a different side of the story.

Similarly, when reporting on a car accident, a journalist would go beyond witness accounts, because witnesses can remember the same event differently. The reporter would interview the police and victims and inspect physical evidence, if possible. If a local resident says there have been five accidents in the same intersection in the last year, the reporter checks public records to see if the statement is true before reporting it.

The same goes for all news stories. A good journalist interviews people on all sides and does research to confirm information. Stories based on thirdhand information, or that only present one side of a story, are not news; they are rumors or opinions.

famous FLUB

On the night of the 2000 U.S. presidential election, the race was so close that all of the major TV networks announced the wrong winner.

The contest between the Democrat, Vice President Al Gore, and the Republican, Texas governor George W. Bush, was so tight that the whole election came down to one state. How would Florida vote?

At 7:50 p.m., NBC called the race for Gore before all of the votes had been counted. The other TV networks panicked and also quickly announced Gore as the winner. Two hours later, the race tightened and all of the networks withdrew the call. Votes were still being counted into the wee hours of the morning, and around 2 a.m., Fox News called the race for Bush. Again, all the networks followed—and then took it back two hours later. At 4 a.m., there was still no winner. And it would take the next five weeks of counting the votes before Bush would be officially announced as the president of the United States.

The front pages of various Texas newspapers reflected the undecided presidential race between Vice President Al Gore and Texas governor George W. Bush in the 2000 presidential election.

THE SPIN Cycle

You know how when you get into trouble, you might try to explain your way out of the situation—maybe by pointing a finger at someone else or by telling a "creative" version of events that makes you look innocent? If this sounds familiar, you may be well practiced in the art of spin—trying to change or control the way others perceive an event. Some people though, like politicians and public figures, do it when talking to the media to squirm their way out of sticky situations. Public relations professionals, sometimes called "spin doctors," create messages for public figures to deliver. They use many of the following techniques to try to shift public opinion.

TRICKS OF THE TRADE

1 **HEY, LOOK OVER THERE!** This technique shifts the conversation away from a negative story and toward a more positive story. A similar technique—called "whataboutism"—is when someone makes a negative comment about another person to avoid addressing a difficult topic. For example, instead of answering a tough question about taxes, a politician might shift the conversation to an opponent: "Well, what about him? He raised everyone's taxes!"

2 **SORRY, NOT SORRY:** Statements like "I'm sorry you feel that way" admit no wrongdoing, and subtly put the blame on the people who were offended—as if they are the ones being unreasonable.

3 **BEND THE FACTS:** Spin doctors often state facts that support a certain viewpoint and leave out the facts that don't support it.

4 **REPEAT LIES UNTIL THEY RING TRUE:** The more often people hear information, the more likely they are to believe it. Spin repeats a story again and again and again ... until the public thinks it's true.

A swirl of magazines at a printing factory

91

RELY ON **Solid Sources**

A responsible journalist follows the "two-source rule." That means confirming a story with two people who have firsthand knowledge of events before the story gets published. Whenever possible, the journalist identifies these sources in the story, including their full names and the company they work for. Similarly, journalists provide source information for all the facts in a story.

In some cases, journalists quote anonymous, or unnamed, sources. This usually happens when publishing sources' names would endanger them or put their job at risk or when the source does not want his or her name attached to the story. One famous anonymous source in history was "Deep Throat," an FBI insider who helped *Washington Post* reporters crack the Watergate scandal—which led President Richard Nixon to step down from office in 1974.

News organizations take anonymity seriously. Sources' identities may be unknown to readers, but they are well known and trusted by the reporters and editors. And journalists have to be willing to protect these sources— otherwise, the reporter and news outlet would lose credibility and public trust, and the reporter's career could be at risk. Sometimes, journalists even choose to go to jail rather than reveal a source to authorities. So reliable news organizations grant anonymity carefully and never do so without good reason.

In June 2005, former FBI deputy director William Mark Felt, pictured here during the Watergate era, revealed that he was the anonymous government source known as "Deep Throat" who helped bring down President Richard Nixon in the Watergate scandal 30 years earlier.

Christiane Amanpour, reporting from a war zone in Bosnia in 1991, is one of television's most well-known news correspondents.

CHRISTIANE AMANPOUR
Reporting From the Danger Zone
(1958–)

A woman with a British-Iranian accent was not a likely candidate to be an on-air reporter back in the 1980s, and a female war correspondent was even more rare. But Christiane Amanpour broke through these boundaries as a reporter for CNN, becoming famous for her reports from Iraq during the Persian Gulf War (1990–91). She became a household name delivering stories from conflict zones around the globe—in Europe, Africa, and the Middle East, among other locations.

Born into a wealthy family, with a British mother and an Iranian father, Amanpour spent her childhood living in both Iran and England. But in 1979, a revolution in Iran forced her family to flee the country and leave behind everything they owned. That experience stayed with Amanpour for the rest of her life and ignited her passion for journalism.

Throughout her career, Amanpour has reported for CNN, ABC News, CBS News, and PBS. In 2017, Amanpour was given her own show, now called *Amanpour and Co.*

(?) Do you think social media sites should be held responsible for distributing false information?

This quote from *Washington Post* editor Ben Bradlee, which hangs on a wall in the center of the paper's newsroom, is a reminder that truth matters.

BE Transparent

Legitimate journalists do their own reporting. And if they must report information from another news organization, they always name the source and credit the media outlet that first reported the scoop. This is common during breaking news situations, such as natural disasters, when the story is still unfolding and information from an official source may not be available.

Journalists work hard to be transparent, meaning they explain what they know and how they know it. News outlets will report when information is incomplete or missing, such as if an important source could not be reached for comment.

Today, journalists are under more pressure than ever to get the story out fast. That means it can be easier to make mistakes. And stories are often published quickly, and then updated as more information comes in.

But it's always better to be accurate than to be fast. Legitimate news organizations have systems in place to ensure quality and catch errors. They hire reliable people, have multiple editors read every story, quiz reporters on their information, and run any negative information by the person who is being criticized. A responsible news organization also tells readers when corrections or updates are made. Look for a time stamp at the top of an online article, which shows when the news was last updated, or a note at the bottom of the story indicating if any changes have been made.

ABOUT
TWO-THIRDS
OF **AMERICANS** GOT
SOME **NEWS ON**
SOCIAL MEDIA
IN **2017**, AND THE NUMBER CONTINUES
TO GROW.

Famous TV journalist Wolf Blitzer hosts CNN's news program *The Situation Room*.

BEWARE OF **Bias**

While many news organizations go to great lengths to get the facts right and report stories fairly, sometimes a reporter will allow personal beliefs (or biases) to get in the way of accuracy. And that's when journalism is no longer responsible. Look out for these signs that a story could be biased.

The words people choose can be biased, such as calling a protester an extremist, which sounds negative, or an activist, which can sound positive. Bias can also lead people to cover certain topics too much and ignore others. Biased reporters may also interview sources who mostly support their viewpoint, leaving out or giving less attention to other opinions.

Another way to show bias is to twist facts into lies by drawing incorrect conclusions. Here's a funny example just to make the point: It's impossible to prove that UFOs don't exist, so they must exist. Obviously, a news reporter would not write that UFOs exist—unless one was actually discovered!—but this type of false logic, in which people leap to incorrect conclusions, is a common form of bias.

ABOVE TOP: TV screens in a newsroom show French president Emmanuel Macron in 2018. **ABOVE BOTTOM:** The Buzzfeed newsroom in Los Angeles, California.

REPUBLICANS ARE MORE LIKELY TO BELIEVE THAT *FOX NEWS* REPORTS NEWS **OBJECTIVELY;** WHILE **DEMOCRATS** ARE MORE SPLIT, MOST OFTEN CHOOSING *CNN AND NPR,* ACCORDING TO A GALLUP/KNIGHT POLL.

The Newseum—a Washington, D.C., museum about news and freedom of the press, which closed in December 2019—displayed the front pages of newspapers from across the country and around the world.

97

THE CODE OF Ethics

The Society of Professional Journalists sets a "code of ethics"—standards to follow—for members of the media. Here are a few of the guidelines from the society's code of ethics and how they impact the choices journalists make every day. Ethical journalism should be accurate and fair, and journalists should be honest and courageous in gathering, reporting, and interpreting information.

SEEK TRUTH AND REPORT IT

SEEK OUT THE SUBJECTS OF NEWS COVERAGE TO ALLOW THEM TO RESPOND TO CRITICISM OR ALLEGATIONS OF WRONGDOING.

WHAT IT MEANS: If a person is going to be accused of doing something bad in a news article, the journalist must give the person every opportunity to respond in the same article by calling, emailing, and in some cases, sending letters.

AVOID STEREOTYPING. JOURNALISTS SHOULD EXAMINE THE WAYS THEIR VALUES AND EXPERIENCES MAY SHAPE THEIR REPORTING.

WHAT IT MEANS: Say a reporter has grown up hearing negative stereotypes about people from a particular cultural background. That could affect how the reporter writes a story involving someone from that same background. Reliable journalists recognize their own biases and let the facts guide the story. Or they sometimes withdraw and let someone else write it, especially if it's about someone they know.

MINIMIZE HARM

Ethical journalism treats sources, subjects, and members of the public as human beings deserving of respect.

BALANCE THE PUBLIC'S NEED FOR INFORMATION AGAINST POTENTIAL HARM AND CONFLICT.

WHAT IT MEANS: When covering a war for example, does a story reveal information that could put a person, or even a whole village, at risk? Journalists must balance the risks of publishing a story with the public's need to know what is happening.

REALIZE THAT PRIVATE PEOPLE HAVE A GREATER RIGHT TO CONTROL INFORMATION ABOUT THEMSELVES THAN PUBLIC FIGURES.

WHAT IT MEANS: Responsible journalists only publish information that's in the public interest and are especially careful when reporting on private citizens. For example, they might choose not to publish where a private citizen lives because the public doesn't need to know that information. But the hometown of a candidate running for a political office is of actual concern to the public because these officials are usually required to live in the town or state they represent.

ACT INDEPENDENTLY

The highest and primary obligation of ethical journalism is to serve the public.

AVOID CONFLICTS OF INTEREST, REAL OR PERCEIVED.

WHAT IT MEANS: Journalists avoid participating in activities that could cause bias or create the impression of bias. If a journalist donates to a politician's campaign, receives a gift from the politician, or participates in a political march, would anyone believe the journalist could write a balanced story about the same politician or the issue that they marched for?

DO NOT PAY FOR ACCESS TO NEWS.

WHAT IT MEANS: Legitimate news organizations never pay people for interviews or information. How would you know if their information is true? Maybe the source is making it up or exaggerating information to make money.

BE ACCOUNTABLE AND TRANSPARENT

Ethical journalism means taking responsibility for one's work and explaining one's decisions to the public.

ACKNOWLEDGE MISTAKES AND CORRECT THEM PROMPTLY AND PROMINENTLY.

WHAT IT MEANS: Journalists should quickly publish corrections and explain what mistakes were made. Corrections should appear where people will clearly see them.

ABIDE BY THE SAME HIGH STANDARD THEY EXPECT OF OTHERS.

WHAT IT MEANS: Journalists should act as role models. To hold others to high standards, you must stick to them yourself.

The host of NBC's news and opinion show *Meet the Press*, Chuck Todd, discusses current events with journalists David Broder and Gwen Ifill.

IS THAT YOUR *Opinion?*

Co-hosts Joe Scarborough, a conservative commentator, and Mika Brzezinski, a liberal commentator, interview then Vice President Joe Biden on their show *Morning Joe*.

Starting in 1987, the TV and radio airwaves unleashed a flood of opinion news shows. Before then, a law called the Fairness Doctrine required radio and TV news to always present both sides of hot-button topics. But when a 1987 court decision overturned the Fairness Doctrine, it wasn't long before big personalities with over-the-top opinions grabbed microphones and started talking and talking ... and they are still talking today.

Radio personalities, such as conservative host Rush Limbaugh,

quickly became celebrities, drawing huge audiences. The more popular the show, the more advertising dollars it attracts. Pretty soon, opinion shows—in which entertaining hosts champion one side of an issue—began delivering sky-high earnings to radio networks. The moneymaking format jumped to television, and today, the most highly rated programs in cable news are opinion shows. Fox News Channel's conservative host Sean Hannity and MSNBC's liberal host Rachel Maddow have two of the most watched programs on cable news channels.

Meanwhile, the explosion of internet news and social media has turned a flood of opinion into a tsunami, with politicians, celebrities, writers, and everyone else—maybe even your relatives—posting opinions about everything from the best pizza flavors to who should run for president. In this swirl of information—much of it looking exactly like news—how can you tell what's what?

ABOVE: Conservative opinion personality Rush Limbaugh
LEFT: Progressive opinion personality Chris Hayes

HEY, THAT'S A HOAX
APRIL **FOOLS**

As an April Fools' Day prank, National Public Radio (NPR)—a major radio news organization—posted this headline on its Facebook page: "Why Doesn't America Read Anymore?" If readers clicked, they landed on a page that revealed the story as a hoax. But a lot of readers commented on the post, sharing their strong opinions about the "story," without ever having read it—proving NPR's point!

?

Do you think you have ever confused opinion and facts?

WHAT IS **Opinion?**

The goal of opinion pieces—on TV as well as in print and online—is to present a particular point of view. Opinion shows on TV can look just like regular news programs, with an "anchorperson," or host, sitting behind a desk, talking about the hot topics of the day. But the purpose of an opinion show is to deliver the host's strong opinion, not unbiased facts.

Breaking news programs, on the other hand, present balanced facts and interviews with people on different sides of a topic. The goal is to help inform the audience. But because news and opinion shows look so similar, it can be hard to tell the difference.

If the host has a giant personality and talks a lot more than anyone else, that's a big clue that you are watching an opinion show. But there are a few other signs as well. First, when you watch regular news programs, the anchorpeople don't express opinions at all. They report straight facts and provide the source of each piece of information. On opinion shows, TV hosts only present facts that support their viewpoint. And the people interviewed either build the host's case or present the opposite viewpoint, only to have the host contradict the guest's argument.

Things get even more confusing when the hosts of opinion shows make guest appearances on news shows. Sometimes a news anchor, who only reports facts, will turn to opinion commentators to get their take on an issue. No wonder viewers are all mixed up.

Opinion is not the same thing as false news, which contains made-up information. Instead, opinion pieces from legitimate news organizations express ideas about true events. However, some hosts on opinion shows—both liberal and conservative—will float theories that stretch the truth, so if something sounds far-fetched, check how other news outlets are reporting on the same topic.

When you turn on the television, it can be difficult to know if you are watching breaking news or an opinion show. Here, in 2019, we see the *Washington Post*'s Bob Woodward as a guest on *The Daily Briefing With Dana Perino*.

The Daily
BRIEFING
★ W/DANA PERINO ★

? Can you think of some big personalities on opinion shows? How can you tell the host's perspective is opinionated?

Funny or Fake?

Studies have found that a lot of people can't tell the difference between false news stories that try to trick people, and satire, which is intended to be funny. Here's how you can tell lies from laughs:

False News

This is entirely or partially untrue information intended to mislead.

Satire

The goal of satire is not to mislead, but rather to entertain and make fun of the flaws of public figures. Comedians such as late-night TV hosts Jimmy Fallon and Stephen Colbert turn current events into jokes for their shows. They mock presidents, world leaders, celebrities—just about anyone in the news is fair game. And satirical websites like The Onion create hilarious false stories that are loosely based on the news, but then take them in crazy directions. These stories do not pretend to be true; their only purpose is to get readers to laugh.

STUDIES HAVE FOUND THAT **PEOPLE** ARE **MORE** LIKELY TO *IDENTIFY AN* **OPINION** *AS A FACT* WHEN **THEY AGREE** WITH **THE OPINION.**

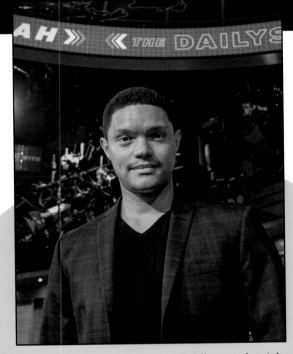

Comedian Trevor Noah delivers a unique take on world events as host of Comedy Central's satire program *The Daily Show.*

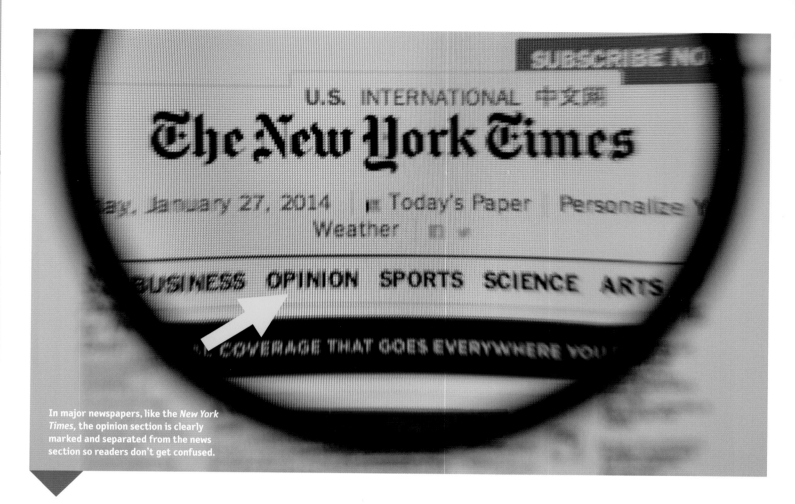

In major newspapers, like the *New York Times*, the opinion section is clearly marked and separated from the news section so readers don't get confused.

Look WHO'S TALKING

Inside major publication newsrooms, opinion writers sit separately from the news writers, and the two sides almost never talk to each other. That's intentional, so one side does not influence the other. Print publications generally label opinion sections clearly. And although legitimate news organizations clearly label opinion pieces online, a 2017 study found that more than half of news websites still don't provide these labels.

Many people are confused. Fewer than half of people surveyed said they could easily tell the difference between news and opinion in online news or social media. So how do you learn to tell one type of article from another? Look for these labels when you read the news. If one of the following labels doesn't appear on a story, but the article fits one of these descriptions, there's a good chance it's an opinion piece:

EDITORIALS represent the opinions of the news organization's editorial board—a team of journalists who write and edit the editorials—and usually do not have a byline (a writer's name) at the top.

COLUMNS are written by regular contributors to a newspaper or website and reflect the opinions of the writer, not the publication. Columnists become personalities who people look forward to reading daily or weekly. Usually the writer's name appears next to a column—sometimes along with the person's photo.

OP-EDS (Opinion-Editorials) are often written by experts from outside the news organization and include information about why the writer is qualified to talk about the topic (usually at the top or bottom of the article). All opinions are those of the writers or the organizations they work for.

LETTERS TO THE EDITOR are written by readers in response to a previously published article.

WHERE DOES *Information* COME FROM?

One of the smartest ways to read news is to always ask yourself, Who is delivering the information? Being able to recognize an opinion piece means you will know when you are reading only one side of an issue. If you want to learn more, you can seek out opinion articles that explain another way of looking at the same topic, or you can look at breaking news stories, which present only the facts. Then you will have balanced information and can make up your mind about what you think is right and wrong.

ARIANNA HUFFINGTON
From the Left
(1950–)

Named one of the world's most powerful women by *Forbes* magazine, Arianna Huffington co-founded the *Huffington Post* in 2005—one of the first liberal-leaning news websites. It began as an opinion blog and grew into a news powerhouse with a left-wing slant. In 2008, the *Observer* newspaper, in London, England, called "HuffPo" the world's most powerful blog.

Surprisingly, Huffington started out on the other side of the fence. She first became famous as a conservative writer and TV commentator and ran for governor of California as an independent (neither a Republican nor a Democrat). Her politics shifted to the left in the 1990s, when she began speaking out in favor of fighting global warming, as well as other progressive causes.

MATT DRUDGE
From the Right
(1966–)

Time.com named Matt Drudge one of the top 25 most influential people on the internet in 2018. His website, called The Drudge Report, is a simple collection of links to news stories and gossip along with some photos, but Drudge's unique taste in news keeps his readers clicking. Drudge considers himself a libertarian, which means he believes the government should have very little involvement in society. But he's an independent thinker who occasionally surprises his conservative followers by supporting a more liberal cause or celebrity.

Drudge became famous in 1998, when he revealed that *Newsweek* magazine was about to break a big story about a scandal. He soon had a TV show on Fox News Channel, which lasted a year, and hosted *Drudge* on WABC radio. His first book, *Drudge Manifesto*, became a best seller.

HE SAID, SHE SAID

Hosts on opinion TV shows can present wildly different arguments. Sometimes, you would hardly even believe they are talking about the same topic. Here's what the liberal *Rachel Maddow Show* on MSNBC and the conservative *Hannity* show—hosted by Sean Hannity—on Fox News had to say about one controversial subject.

THE DEBATE

President Trump wants to build a bigger border wall between Mexico and the United States. Trump and his supporters argue that the wall will keep out drugs and prevent immigrants from entering the United States illegally. People who oppose the wall believe it will be a waste of money and that there are better ways to accomplish the same goal. Here's what the talk show hosts on either side had to say about it:

SEAN HANNITY:

"You witnessed President Trump make a powerful, compelling case for the wall on our southern border. This is a national emergency. The situation is now dire. And whether or not we secure our border, it does have real life-or-death consequences."

RACHEL MADDOW:

From the Rachel Maddow blog: "Trump insists there's a 'crisis' that apparently only he can see … Trump insists that to oppose a wall is to welcome crime, but there's ample evidence that undocumented immigrants are less likely to break American laws than native citizens."

GOING TO EXTREMES

How is it possible for two people to have such different opinions about the same topic? That's the hosts' job. They attract viewers who share their political beliefs, taking stories to the extreme and playing to viewers' emotions. It's a formula that scores big audiences and big bucks for the TV networks. But, in reality, the truth almost always sits somewhere between the extremes.

HOW DO YOU KNOW WHAT TO BELIEVE?

The first step is to read or watch stories about immigration from several well-respected newspapers or news sites. Notice whether the stories are news or opinion pieces. You will likely find that the topic is much more complicated than the opinion hosts make it sound.

As you explore, see if you can find answers to basic questions about the issue: Why do immigrants want to come to the United States? How do they usually enter the country? What are some of the pros and cons of a border wall?

FACT-CHECK THE TV HOSTS

Hannity and Maddow debate whether immigrants pose a threat to U.S. safety. Why take Hannity's or Maddow's word for it, when you can find out for yourself? Do an internet search on some of the facts that both hosts use. If news sites pop up, what sources do they include for the information? Are they reliable sources, such as expert organizations?

If you are unfamiliar with the organization behind the facts and feel like digging deeper, go to its website and click on the "About Us" link to see what the group is all about. Next, look up "national emergency" and "undocumented immigrant," or any other terms you want to learn more about.

MAKE YOUR OWN DECISION

List pros and cons on both sides of the argument, based on what you've learned. If you already have strong ideas about the subject, be careful to be as unbiased as possible in making your list. Think like a reporter and let the facts tell you the real story.

Now, the next time you hear a story that sounds a little too extreme to be true, you can use this formula and the tips from this chapter to discover the truth.

Rachel Maddow

Sean Hannity

Construction crews working on a section of replacement border wall along the border between the U.S. and Mexico, 2019

107

SHOW ME THE Money

Want to share a funny video or research your favorite sports team's stats? The internet is your best friend! A quick search pops up hundreds, even thousands, of pages of information. You can read free stories and watch free videos until your eyes cross—or it's time for bed. But did you ever stop to think about who funds all of the content that is created or who determines what stories you see?

WHO **Pays** FOR NEWS?

News organizations pay highly trained journalists to report and write articles. They also have to pay for the buildings that house their offices and all of the computers and technology needed to publish. Print publications also pay for printing presses, paper, ink, and so on. So where does the money they need come from?

Some news organizations require readers to pay for subscriptions. And, while subscriptions are increasing overall, even that doesn't bring in enough money to keep the lights on. Most news is funded largely through advertising. That's true for print and online news, as well as for most news on TV and the radio.

On many websites, like National Geographic, readers must get subscriptions to have access to all content on the site.

EVERY MONTH AT Costa Rica's Ostional National Wildlife Refuge, tens to hundreds of thousands of female sea turtles arrive, often within a few days of each other, to lay their eggs on the beach.

Biologist Vanessa Bézy has been studying this remarkable phenomenon, known as a mass arrival, or *arribada* in

You have **5 free articles** left this month.

Exploration is just a click away.
Subscribe to get unlimited access to National Geographic and a free tote.

SUBSCRIBE NOW

immense gathering of the creatures— the greatest density of sea turtle species ever recorded.

"I immediately knew there was

How do you get your news? Is it the same way the rest of your family does? Your friends?

108

Undercover ADS

You know an ad when you see one, right? Well, not so fast. If your favorite celebrity blogger or Instagram star raves about a certain soft drink, would you think it was an ad? There's a good chance that the beverage company paid for that person to mention the product. Ads like these are called "sponsored content," and they are disguised to look genuine.

Sponsored content often draws viewers in with fun information and then promotes a product within an article or social media post. A recent study found that some 82 percent of middle schoolers couldn't tell the difference between sponsored content and a real news story online. Here's why: Ads on television and online can be obvious when a show or video stops and an ad begins. In a print newspaper or magazine, ads often appear on separate pages or in boxes on the same page. They are designed to look different from the other pages, making them easy to spot. Some are labeled as "special advertising sections" at the top or bottom of the page.

Other online ads are impossible to miss, like those pop-ups that block the page when you are trying to read. And you probably recognize "banner ads" that run across the top, bottom, or side of a page, often with a video or moving images.

But here's where things get tricky: Sponsored content is also a type of paid advertising, but it looks like a regular article or social media post. Responsible news sites label these pages as "sponsored content" or "advertisements," usually above or below the headline. But on many sites, sponsored content may not be labeled at all. If you see a product or service advertised within a story or on social media, there's a good chance someone paid for that information to be there.

I Spy a Product Placement

News stories aren't the only places you'll see hidden ads. Movies and TV shows are filled with sponsored content as well. In the blockbuster movie *Jurassic World,* Owen, the velociraptor trainer, rolls up to the dinosaur theme park in a sleek Mercedes Benz. In the movie *Teenage Mutant Ninja Turtles,* the pizza-loving characters scarf down pies from Pizza Hut. These brands don't just appear in movies by accident. Advertisers pay big money for product placements—when movies, TV shows, and social media platforms include certain brands in their story lines. Advertisers even pay internet celebrities to wear certain brands of clothing in their videos or include specific products in their social media posts.

Product placements are everywhere. One study found that some 64 percent of movies contained at least one brand placement. So next time your favorite character takes a swig of a soft drink with a big logo on the front, there's a good chance that the beverage company paid thousands of dollars for the promotion. Product placements can pop up just about anywhere, so stay on the lookout for those undercover ads in all kinds of media.

Jurassic World, 2015

SEARCH AND Rescue

Internet searches are also full of sponsored content. Of course it's tempting to click on the first link that pops up in an online search. Surely, the most important links are at the top, right? Well, not exactly. The first links that show up are almost always labeled "sponsored content." If you look closely, you can sometimes see a little button that simply says "Ad." That means a company has paid the search engine to make sure you see its link before anyone else's. Sometimes paid ads fill almost the whole first page of search results. This formula rakes in the cash for companies such as Google, which, together with Facebook, receives half of all the money companies spend on internet advertising.

And even once you get past the sponsored links, a number of factors determine which web pages rise to the top of your search. One of them is the number of clicks a site has received. To find information you can trust, look for sites that you recognize or links from reputable organizations or news sources—even if you have to click to the second or third page of search results to find them.

WHO **Owns** THE NEWS?

While advertisers pour more money into online content, print newspapers are struggling to stay afloat. The internet has taken the greatest toll on local newspapers, which relied on income mostly from classifieds—ads for job openings, cars, homes, and many other items. Now free websites are devoted to job listings and car and home sales, so there's no need to run these ads in the local paper.

As independent newspapers have fallen on hard times, big media companies have swooped in to buy them, closing many newspapers and shrinking others. In fact, today three media companies own over 900 newspapers in the United States, and most own TV networks, online news sites, radio stations, book publishers, and other internet businesses, too.

This has some media experts worried that too few people control too much of the news in the United States and around the world. They are concerned that businesspeople, not editors, may decide which articles are published. Media owners at less professional news outlets may favor certain stories because they attract ad dollars, or squash stories that could offend a sponsor. Additionally, when a few giant companies own most of the news, fewer voices are represented, which can decrease the amount of coverage from under-represented people like women and people of color. Top news organizations, however, have strict rules in place to make sure advertisers don't influence their stories.

FACEBOOK ALSO OWNS *INSTAGRAM, WHATSAPP,* AND THE **VIRTUAL REALITY** COMPANY *OCULUS VR,* AMONG OTHER COMPANIES.

Where do people get local news in your town?

LACK OF **Local News**

Ownership by a few big companies also means that most journalism jobs in the United States and many other countries are now in big cities. Local papers that still exist are often owned and controlled by people in distant cities who know little about specific communities. And there are no longer enough local reporters to cover state and local lawmakers, businesses, and courthouses in smaller towns and cities. When journalists aren't watching, it's easier for local government officials to get away with bad behavior.

After retiring from the *Washington Post,* newspaper editor James Russell Wiggins bought *The Ellsworth American,* a small-town weekly newspaper in Maine, U.S.A. He transformed the paper into a nationally recognized publication.

Digital technology, wireless connectivity, smartphones, and other technological advances have dramatically changed how people gather and access the news.

THE NEW Frontier OF NEWS

The media business keeps changing, and some people are now challenging this big-media model. Several wealthy families and individuals have purchased news organizations, putting off short-term profits to restore quality to the news. Amazon owner and billionaire Jeff Bezos purchased the *Washington Post* in Washington, D.C., and media mogul Patrick Soon-Shiong purchased the struggling *Los Angeles Times* in California. He says he is determined to return the paper to its former glory as a leading national newspaper. The Ochs-Sulzberger family has owned the *New York Times* since 1896, and has resisted the industry trend to sell to a bigger company.

Some nonprofit news organizations are popping up. Being nonprofit means that they are funded by donations instead of advertising. These organizations, such as *ProPublica* and *Texas Tribune*, focus on reporting and telling stories they think are most important, without having to worry about making a profit.

The only thing that seems to remain unchanged in the media business is the public's thirst for news. So, although the last 10 years have been a bumpy road for the industry, the business will carry on.

Choose YOUR NEWS

While many see downsides to big media, some argue that there are benefits as well. With so many different businesses under one roof, these corporations can create TV shows and web content to suit different interests.

Viewers and readers now have many more choices for how they receive their news: in print, on TV, on computers or mobile devices, or through social media. And because these large corporations own profitable TV and movie businesses, they sometimes support the less profitable print and online news business, helping to keep the news alive. Similarly, big media organizations have the resources to cover major national and international stories and send reporters across the globe to report on critical human stories—on everything from hunger to human rights violations—that would otherwise fly under the radar.

CATCHING A SIGNAL

112

Why is everyone standing on a beach, holding their cell phones to the sky? They are trying to phone home.

National Geographic photographer John Stanmeyer took this picture along the shores of the Red Sea, in an African country called Djibouti. He told *National Geographic* the story behind this surprising and beautiful shot: "While [walking] along the beach, I came upon a group of people at dusk, all standing at different spots along the shoreline holding up their phones." The photographer found out that the people are mostly from the neighboring country of Somalia, and often come to this spot to do what is called "catching"—to catch an inexpensive signal from Somalia. If they were lucky enough to pick up a signal, they could Skype with their families at home at a much cheaper rate.

"Some would stand in one place for 20 or 30 minutes, waiting for their phone to grab the faint signal," Stanmeyer says. "It felt as if I was photographing all of us ... trying to connect to our loved ones."

With news coming from so many sources, it can be difficult to know which sources to trust.

Finding
the TRUTH

Most of us want to know what's going on in our hometown or around the world. If you are reading a trustworthy newspaper or watching reliable TV news, you can usually be confident that the stories have been fact-checked and are true. But when we get news from social media or a video or website, it can be hard to tell where the information came from. How do you know if the story originated from a legitimate news source, or if someone just made it up?

WHAT CAN YOU Trust?

People get tricked all the time. Experiments conducted by a scientist from the Massachusetts Institute of Technology (MIT) found that adults believe news that is untrue about 20 percent of the time. And it's even tougher for kids. Some 44 percent of kids say they can't tell fake stories from real ones, according to a 2017 poll by Common Sense Media. So why are we so easily fooled? And how can we avoid sharing false information? This chapter will give you the tools to tell fact from fiction, and it might even help you kick the clicking habit.

A statue of an alien greets visitors to the Alien Research Center, located near the U.S. Air Force's Area 51 facility in the Nevada desert. False theories about aliens have swirled around this spot since 1947.

You can find stories about anything on the internet, including stories in which people claim to have seen Bigfoot, also known as Sasquatch. Fact or fiction?

SASQUATCH X-ING

IN ONE POLL, **69%** OF *TWEENS AND TEENS* SAID THEY PAY **"A LOT"** OR **"SOME" ATTENTION** TO THE **SOURCES OF NEWS** ON SOCIAL MEDIA.

MARK ZUCKERBERG
King of Social Media
(1984–)

Co-founder and CEO of Facebook, Zuckerberg built a social networking site—originally called The Facebook—from his college dorm room at Harvard University in Massachusetts, U.S.A. After his second year, Zuckerberg left school to work on the site full-time. By the end of 2004, the site had a million users. At first, the social network was available to only college students, but slowly Zuckerberg made it available to everyone age 13 and older. Today, more than two billion people around the world are on Facebook, and Zuckerberg is one of the world's richest people.

Facebook has come under fire for allegedly selling private information about its users without their knowledge and for allowing false news stories to be widely distributed on the site. Zuckerberg has taken some steps to tackle both problems, but many say it is not enough.

Facebook also bought Instagram and WhatsApp and now makes more money than any other social network. In 2019, Facebook co-founder Chris Hughes, who no longer works for the company, said the social network had become too powerful and called for the U.S. government to break it up into several smaller companies. That hasn't happened yet, but the future may hold big changes for Facebook.

Following THE CROWD

Human brains are wired to trust information that everyone else trusts. If a story has been shared a gazillion times before, that makes us want to share it, too.

Kids are even more likely to believe stories that come from family members. You trust the person who sent it, so you trust the story. That makes sense. But most people have accidentally shared a false story at some point.

And if an article includes a picture or video, that's just another cue to our brains that we should believe it. How could a story be wrong when the proof is right in front of our eyes? Most of the time that instinct is correct, but digitally altered photos and videos can sometimes fake us out.

Plus, the more shocking the stories and images are, the faster people react to them. So before you share a story or photo, stop to question whether it actually makes sense.

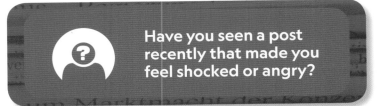

Have you seen a post recently that made you feel shocked or angry?

According to the National Cyber Security Alliance, 49 percent of teens are "very" or "somewhat" concerned that they will mistakenly spread false news over the internet.

GUT Feelings

Psychologists have found that we respond to shocking stories because people often follow their emotions more than logic. Outrageous headlines trigger strong feelings—we laugh, our faces turn red with anger, we shout "No way!" out loud to no one but our screens. Of course, we're going to click and read more. And often, we share the story with everyone we know.

Plus, psychologists have found that when people are overloaded with information, they take mental shortcuts. They choose something familiar—a brand they know or a news story about someone they voted for—over something new.

You know what it's like, you're watching a funny video, doing homework, and getting text messages from your friends all at once. It's hard to know what to focus on. The thing that's the most familiar and makes you feel good, like a text from your best friend, is most likely to get your attention. It's similar with social media posts. People are more likely to believe stories that give them that positive, familiar feeling, even if the information isn't true.

Next time you go online, pay attention to what you read, and see if you are more likely to click on stories that make you feel shocked or happy.

What Is Clickbait?

Websites and social media are full of shocking headlines. These are called clickbait, because they are designed to lure you in—like a fish to bait—so you'll click on the link. Clickbait comes in many forms, as funny or surprising articles or as scams. It could be crazy headlines, strange videos or GIFs, weird photos, or anything that screams "You've won!" or "Share this!" But if the link takes you to a page with no content or an article that doesn't live up to the headline, you've been caught, hook, line, and sinker. What's the point? The website makes money every time someone clicks. Sometimes, messages like these are major warnings that a website might be a scam or put a virus on your computer. Stop before you click. Restart your computer or mobile phone instead.

HEY, THAT'S A HOAX!
WILD ANIMALS **TERRORIZE** NEW YORK

Sensational headlines have always attracted—and fooled—readers, even before clickbait existed. Check out this one from November 9, 1874: "Awful Calamity: Wild Animals Broken Loose from Central Park." The *New York Herald* reported that an angry rhinoceros at the Central Park Zoo had bashed through its cage and then smashed up the other animals' cages. According to the story, the dangerous beasts had all escaped and were running wild through New York City. A lion was spotted inside a church. A sea lion and a rhinoceros were seen fighting in the zoo. The hospitals were full of wounded people, and 49 people were already dead. New Yorkers were terrified.

But there was a catch. At the end of the story, a note from the editors said it was made up. "Not one word of it is true," they wrote, but few read that far in the article. The story did, however, accomplish the editors' goal of getting the broken animal cages repaired at the Central Park Zoo. No legitimate newspaper would publish a story like this today, but at the time, no stunt seemed too far-fetched if it would attract more readers or achieve a goal.

Breaking THE BUBBLE

Social media sites build upon positive feelings so that you will keep coming back. The sites track what you click on, which posts you "like" or "heart," and what you respond to most. They use this information to automatically feed you more of what you like and less of what you don't, so you'll stay on the site and keep clicking and sharing.

Instead of being introduced to new ideas, you get more information about what you already know. Say you are a huge basketball fan and love following your favorite players on social media, the social site will send you more basketball information. But you probably won't see many stories about hockey or horseback riding camp, unless you suddenly start "liking" stories about those topics.

It's no big deal if you read about only one sport, but when it comes to news, people tend to read only news they agree with. And, as you read in chapter 3, we are all more likely to believe information that confirms our beliefs. So if the social media bubble sends someone false information that echoes what they already believe to be true, they may be more likely to be fooled. To pop the bubble, people need to leave their social media feeds and read reliable news and information from many different sources, especially if a social media story looks too strange to be true.

A STUDY FOUND THAT *YOUNG PEOPLE* ARE AMONG THE MOST LIKELY TO READ CLICKBAIT.

EVAN SPIEGEL
Inventor of Snapchat
(1990–)

Who's behind the wacky images you send your friends on Snapchat? Evan Spiegel and two college classmates, Reggie Brown and Bobby Murphy, who created a disappearing message app in 2011, as students at Stanford University, in California.

They launched the app in July of that year with the name Picaboo. But after the business partners had a falling out, Brown left the company, and Spiegel and Murphy renamed the app, calling it Snapchat. It was so successful that Spiegel, Brown, and Murphy became billionaires in their 20s!

In 2015, Snapchat introduced the "Discover" feature, which provides news videos and other programs from CNN, BuzzFeed, the *Washington Post*, and Mashable, among other sources. The verdict is still out on whether this will be a reliable way to get news or a passing trend.

The Truth
Tool Kit

It's easy to fall for falsehoods, but you can outsmart the fakers. Next time a story makes you raise an eyebrow, break out this tool kit. Asking these questions will make you an expert at telling truth from fiction.

WHAT IS THE SOURCE?

Look beyond who shared the story with you, because sometimes even friends and family accidentally share false stories. The best way to find out if a post is accurate is to look at the source of the information. If you recognize the publication it comes from and have found it to be trustworthy in the past, or if it's the web page of a major newspaper, magazine, or TV news network, it's generally reliable. If not, follow the tips below to keep digging.

IS THE STORY OUTRAGEOUS?

Does the story sound too wild to believe? Is it so far-fetched that you can't imagine it even happened? Is it too good to be true? Then it may not have happened at all. Read all the way through to the end of the article, and check to see if reliable news sites are reporting the same story.

IS IT FULL OF TYPOS?

If you see a lot of misspelled words, incorrect grammar, or other typos—that's a sure sign that it is not from a legitimate news source. Look at other sources to check it out.

DOES IT LOOK LIKE A SUPERMARKET TABLOID?

Does the headline appear in all capital letters, or do you see wacky-looking pictures of famous people—perhaps their appearance is much different from what you have seen in the past? Are there aliens in the photo? Are there a lot of exclamation marks in the headlines? If so, that's a warning that a story shouldn't be trusted.

DO YOU FEEL ANGRY OR SHOCKED?

Made-up stories are designed to make you feel strong emotions so you will click and share them instantly. When you are overwhelmed with emotion, it's easy not to notice that an article is missing a lot of facts. Next time a headline makes you mad before you've even read the first line of the story, take a deep breath and look to see if the sources of the information are in the story.

ARE EXPERTS QUOTED?

Legitimate news stories will attribute all facts and quotes. This means articles will include where information comes from and identify the people quoted. If an anonymous, or unnamed, source is quoted, the reporter will explain why the person is not identified. Think twice if an article includes no sources or only has experts who speak to one side of the story.

FALSE STORIES TRAVEL SIX TIMES *FASTER* ON **TWITTER** THAN REAL STORIES DO.

WHAT IS THE PURPOSE OF THE STORY?

If it seems like the article is written with the intent to either harm or promote a certain group of people, that's a sign that you are reading propaganda rather than news.

IS IT BREAKING NEWS?

As natural disasters or other breaking news stories unfold, journalists report the news as it happens—especially on live TV. Journalists do the best they can, but the very first information they report could be inaccurate. So if you hear phrases like "We are getting reports that ...," or "We have not been able to independently verify ...," these facts may turn out not to be true. Check back later for the full story.

ARE POP-UPS CAUSING PROBLEMS?

Many websites have pop-up ads. Annoying? Yes! But not necessarily a sign that anything is wrong with a website. If you see ads with bright, flashing colors or a spinning wheel that pops up in the middle of the page, consider exiting or shutting down your computer right away. It could be a scam, or it might give your computer a virus.

121

HOW TO BE AN EXPERT FACT-CHECKER

If you use the truth tool kit on the previous pages and are still uncertain about whether a story is accurate, pretend you're a detective and keep digging. Where do you go next? Professional fact-checkers—who make sure stories are correct before they are published—say that looking outside the story is the real secret to success. Use these truth-telling tips to tell if a story is for real.

SEARCH THE **EXACT HEADLINE.**

Type the exact same title of the story into a search engine. If the story isn't real, websites may pop up right away that call it out as fake.

LOOK FOR OTHER ARTICLES ON THE **SAME TOPIC.**

Big news stories will be covered by most major news organizations. If a story seems hard to believe, and it only pops up in one or two places, that's a warning sign that something's wrong.

CHECK **THE DATE.**

Is this a new story, or did it happen a long time ago? If it isn't current, the information may be incorrect or just out of date.

SEE IF IT'S A **KNOWN HOAX.**

Many websites are dedicated to snuffing out incorrect stories and urban legends (myths that everyone thinks are true). If a story sounds suspicious, ask an adult to help you look it up on a site that specializes in finding hoaxes, such as Snopes.com, PolitiFact.com, FactCheck.org, or Hoax-Slayer.net.

NATIONAL GEOGRAPHIC

A camera trap near Yellowstone National Park catches a grizzly bear stealing whitebark pine nuts from a squirrel's cache. The nuts are an important food for the bears, which are omnivorous.

PHOTOGRAPH BY DREW RUSH, NAT GEO IMAGE COLLECTION

ANIMALS | YELLOWSTONE LIVE

The most bizarre things grizzly bears eat, from elk to moths

These famously hungry omnivores have been shown to eat an astonishing variety of plants and animals.

3 MINUTE READ

BY **DOUGLAS MAIN**

PUBLISHED JUNE 25, 2019

WEST YELLOWSTONE— What won't grizzlies eat?

In the Greater Yellowstone Great Ecosystem, grizzlies will eat just about every animal that lives in the region, if given the chance. In a surprising moment on Monday's episode of *Yellowstone Live*, on the National Geographic Channel, a

ABOUT A THIRD OF KIDS WHO SHARED A *NEWS STORY* SAID THEY LATER FOUND OUT IT WAS *FAKE* OR INACCURATE.

DOUBLE-CHECK **THE EXPERTS.**
Search the experts quoted in the story to learn more about the organizations they represent. Are the experts qualified to speak about the topic? Do the organizations they work for represent a certain point of view? And if so, are experts with differing points of view included in the story? If the article is one-sided, that's a sign of potentially biased reporting.

GO STRAIGHT TO **THE SOURCE.**
A reliable news story should say where all the facts came from. Search the internet to look for the organizations behind the facts. Do they have a particular bias? For example, if an organization that represents peanut growers is behind a study about the health benefits of peanut butter, you know the goal is to sell more peanut butter.

VERIFY IT.
Many social media sites flag the real accounts of famous people or well-known organizations. Look for check marks, icons, or even special emojis next to the account names that show they have been verified. Some fake social media accounts will try to trick people with similar marks elsewhere on the page. If it's not right next to the account name, it's probably a phony.

GET **UNSTUCK.**
Social media is designed to keep you on the site. If you think something's fishy about a story, leave the social media site and look up the story on a search engine to look for other sources. Also try searching in a new browser or clearing your history, so your search history can't follow you.

BE A **SEARCH ENGINE** GENIUS.
As you read earlier, the first websites that pop up in internet searches are often ads. Sometimes these are marked as ads; sometimes they aren't. Before you click, scan at least the first two pages of results and read the few lines of description underneath each link. Click on the website of an organization that you recognize or that seems most expert on the subject you are researching.

SIGNS THAT A WEBSITE IS Fake

It's one thing to fact-check an article, but what if a whole website seems fishy? Fact-checking pros also have secret strategies for detecting websites that are not what they pretend to be. Ask an adult to help you do some research. Sometimes you have to go beyond the words to look closely at the site itself.

Check THE URL (THE WEBSITE'S LINK, OR "ADDRESS").

- Trustworthy website addresses end in .com for companies, .net for private networks, .edu for educational institutions, .org for nonprofit organizations, .gov for government sites, and .mil for military sites.

- If a website originates in a country other than the United States, the two-letter abbreviation for the country appears at the end of the URL. For example, .uk for the United Kingdom (including England), or .fr for France.

- If a URL ends in .co, .lo, com.com, or .com.lo, instead of the usual .com, the site is probably a phony.

- If a URL has been shortened, so you can't see the original source, you can "unshorten" it at unshorten.it or checkshorturl .com/expand.php.

Look FOR AN "ABOUT US" LINK.

Websites for real organizations or companies tell you what they do and who is behind the site. Look for an "About Us" link or tab at the top or very bottom (sometimes in tiny type) of the home page. When you've read who they are, consider if you've learned enough. Perhaps after reading the description, you'll need to do an internet search on the company name to find out who owns the organization and who they work with.

Expect HIGH-QUALITY IMAGES.

Many reliable news sources pride themselves on strong photography. If images are blurry or show pictures of people making strange faces, think twice about the information on the site.

BE ON Logo Patrol.

Fake websites can be almost exact copies of websites for well-known organizations. If your "Spidey sense" is telling you that something doesn't feel right, look closely at the company logo to see if it's the real deal or just a close copy of the original. Be on the lookout for small differences, like two letters switched around, if one color of the logo has been altered, or other small changes with the branding.

Have you ever been fooled by a fake logo?

Always double-check information you find online, especially on crowdsourced sites such as Wikipedia.

When to Wiki It

When you write a paper for school, is Wikipedia the first place you look? That's OK as a first step, but it's important to confirm what you find on Wiki in other sources. Here's why: Wikipedia is not the same as a regular encyclopedia, which is written and edited by professionals. Instead, anyone with access to the internet can write and edit entries in Wikipedia. Volunteers run Wikipedia in an attempt to help people share their knowledge with others around the globe. And although studies have found that Wiki can be as accurate as professional encyclopedias, there are also many cases in which people have posted incorrect information on the site. Sometimes people post false information on the Wiki page of a celebrity or public figure they don't like. People can also accidentally post information that's wrong.

That doesn't mean you cannot use Wikipedia. You'll often find links to other, reliable sources at the bottom of a Wiki page. But if you do use the site, check the information you find in at least two reliable sources, such as professional encyclopedias, websites of known organizations, books, or news reports.

JEFF BEZOS
Tech Giant and Media Mogul
(1964–)

As this book goes to press, the richest man in the United States is Jeff Bezos, who launched Amazon.com out of his garage in 1994. What began as an online bookstore has turned into the world's largest internet shopping site. The company is also behind Kindle e-readers and Amazon Prime Video—the successful movie and TV streaming service—among other businesses. Bezos also owns a company called Blue Origin that's developing rockets to carry passengers into space. But in 2013, the tech genius did something that seemed very old-fashioned for a technology leader. He bought a newspaper.

Bezos paid $250 million for the *Washington Post,* one of the nation's leading newspapers. The highly respected Washington, D.C.–based paper had been struggling financially for years. Bezos saw an opportunity to use his digital expertise to reach more readers. By 2016, the *Washington Post* had become profitable under his leadership.

125

famous FLUB

OLD STORY, NEW PROBLEM

In 2008, an employee at a U.S. financial firm in Miami, Florida, U.S.A., thought she had spotted big news. She had read a story online that a major U.S. airline had filed for bankruptcy. That meant the company was in big financial trouble and might have to close. She forwarded the news report to a major news service, which then sent the story to its subscribers in the financial industry. Within 15 minutes, the stock for the airline tanked, causing the value of the company to plunge. The only problem was that the news story was six years old.

The article had no date on it, so when it popped up at the top of a Google search, it was easy to mistake for a current story. After the error was discovered, the airline's stock bounced back, and the airline demanded that the *South Florida Sun-Sentinel,* which published the original story in 2002, remove the article from its website.

OUT-OF-PLACE *Photos*

A social media post falsely claimed that trash piled on this lawn in Georgia, U.S.A., had been left by people attending an Earth Day celebration in California.

Seeing isn't always believing. Real photos are sometimes paired with fake stories, tricking readers into thinking a story is true—because there's even a photo to prove it. Here are some examples of out-of-place photos that spawned fake stories.

LITTERBUGS

THE RUMOR: A group of environmentalists in California supposedly left tons of litter behind after an Earth Day celebration in 2019. The accusation is shocking because it suggests the environmentalists don't actually care about Earth.

WHAT'S REAL: A real photo of litter got the rumor started, but the photo was taken in 2009 in Georgia.

THE FULL STORY: The photo was posted on social media in March 2019, with a caption blaming the mess on the Earth Day event. Thousands of people shared the post, even though Earth Day is on April 22, and hadn't even happened yet. The image was actually taken 10 years earlier and had appeared in several news stories about spectators at a University of Georgia football game who had left behind some 70 tons of trash. The Earth Day event in California never actually happened.

126

WORLD'S MOST GENEROUS LOTTERY WINNER

THE RUMOR: A 2018 tweet from Florida lottery winner Shane Missler promised to give $5,000 to the first 50,000 people who liked and retweeted his post.

WHAT'S REAL: The photo of Missler that appeared with the tweet.

THE FULL STORY: The message even came from a social media account in Missler's name, with his picture on it. But the whole thing was a hoax. Some sneaky person copied a photo of Missler found online and created a false account for him. In this case, if it sounds too good to be true, it is!

MUTANT FLOWERS

THE RUMOR: In May 2015, a photo of "mutant" daisies growing near a Japanese nuclear power plant—which had suffered a meltdown in 2011—circulated on social media. The writer included the radiation levels of the soil in his post, and the social media universe exploded. People went bonkers, assuming the deformed daisies, with two flower bulbs merged into one, had mutated as a result of radiation from the plant.

WHAT'S REAL: The power plant had actually suffered a meltdown following an earthquake and tsunami. The photo of the Frankenstein flowers was real, and they really did grow in Japan about 108 miles (174 km) from the nuclear power plant.

THE FULL STORY: Plant experts quickly jumped into the conversation to explain that flowers with the bulbs joined together grow in many different locations. The radiation in the soil was considered at a safe level, and there was no evidence that radiation had caused the mutation. Numerous scientists and fact-checking websites corrected the rumor, but three years later, it was still circulating on popular social media sites.

Mutated daisies, like this one, can appear around the world.

LEARN TO DETECT
Phony Photos

Technology has made it so easy to alter photos that it can be hard even for professionals to tell if a photo is real or fake. Some experts specialize in "photo forensics," using special software to detect false photos. But you can use these simple tricks to tell if a photo might be a fake:

1   Look at the shadows. The light should be on one side and the shadows should be on the other. And all of the shadows should be at the same angle. If the shadows look off, that's a sign that something may have been altered.

2   Does someone's head look too big, or is a person's body positioned at a strange angle? That could be a sign that two images have been combined into one.

3   Does it look like anything in the photo has been duplicated, with the same image appearing more than once?

4   If a photo looks suspicious, try doing a reverse image search. The search will show you where else the image has appeared online. If it shows up with details that are different from the ones you are seeing, that's a sign that the photo is doctored.

CAN YOU FIGURE OUT WHAT IS PHONY IN THE FOLLOWING PHOTOS?

A

B

C

ANSWERS: A. The same flower is repeated multiple times, and did you notice the duplicated clouds? B. This shot is missing shadows, and the people are too big in relation to the mountain. C. The fireworks are drawn in and seem to come out of the ground. Look closely, you'll see mountains in the background. But this is Brandenburg Gate, located in Berlin, Germany—a big city that's not near a mountain range. D. These grizzly bears look "pasted" into the scene. They don't look natural. E. This cuddly panda mother and cub sure are sweet, but they appear cut out and placed in this bamboo setting. F. Several duplicate groups of people are sitting on the grass.

QUIZ: Real OR Fake?

NOW THAT YOU KNOW WHAT TO LOOK OUT FOR, LET'S SEE IF YOU CAN PUT YOUR TRUTH TOOL KIT AND NEW PHOTO SMARTS INTO ACTION. TAKE THIS QUIZ TO TEST-DRIVE YOUR NEW SKILLS. SOME QUESTIONS MAY HAVE MORE THAN ONE CORRECT ANSWER. CHOOSE ALL THAT APPLY.

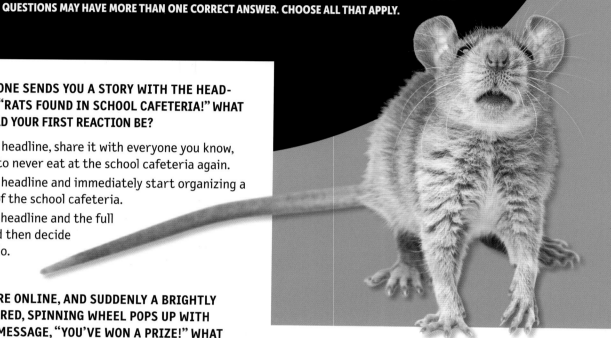

1 SOMEONE SENDS YOU A STORY WITH THE HEADLINE, "RATS FOUND IN SCHOOL CAFETERIA!" WHAT SHOULD YOUR FIRST REACTION BE?

a. Read the headline, share it with everyone you know, and vow to never eat at the school cafeteria again.

b. Read the headline and immediately start organizing a protest of the school cafeteria.

c. Read the headline and the full story, and then decide what to do.

2 YOU'RE ONLINE, AND SUDDENLY A BRIGHTLY COLORED, SPINNING WHEEL POPS UP WITH THE MESSAGE, "YOU'VE WON A PRIZE!" WHAT SHOULD YOUR FIRST REACTION BE?

a. Awesome! A prize! You click on the link and fill in your name and email address.

b. You close the window immediately; it could be a scam or computer virus.

c. There's no back button, so you click to see what will happen.

3 YOU DISCOVER THAT YOU ACCIDENTALLY SHARED A FALSE STORY ON SOCIAL MEDIA, WHAT SHOULD YOU DO?

a. Nothing. It was just for fun, anyway.

b. Tell only your family and best friends. They'll understand, and anyway you're way too embarrassed to tell everyone you shared it with.

c. Reshare the story to the same people you sent it to the first time, but this time, tell them you found out it's a fake. Ask them to send out a similar correction if they shared the story with others.

4 AN AWESOME PHOTO CIRCULATED ON SOCIAL MEDIA. COULD IT POSSIBLY BE REAL? WHAT CAN YOU DO TO FIND OUT?

a. Do a reverse image search on Google or another search engine and see where else the image appears.

b. Don't bother checking it. It's obviously real; otherwise, how could there even be a picture?

c. See if any of the fact-checking websites have called out the image as a hoax.

5 YOU SEE A POST ON YOUR FAVORITE CELEBRITY'S SOCIAL MEDIA ACCOUNT. SHE'S SAYING REALLY WEIRD STUFF TODAY—SHE DOESN'T EVEN SOUND LIKE HERSELF. WHAT DO YOU DO?

a. Share the post with all of your friends. This is pretty entertaining.

b. Check to see if this is the celebrity's real account. Look for a check mark or other symbol next to her account name to verify the account is real.

c. Nothing. Celebrities act strange sometimes.

6

YOU ARE BROWSING A WELL-KNOWN NEWS WEBSITE, BUT SOMETHING SEEMS OFF. THE STORIES LOOK STRANGE, AND THE WEBSITE DOESN'T LOOK VERY PROFESSIONAL. HOW CAN YOU CHECK IF IT'S REAL?

a. Look at the URL to see if has a strange ending, like .lo or .co instead of .com.

b. Notice if the site has a lot of misspellings or typos.

c. Do a new internet search on the company's name to see what the news organization's logo looks like on other sites. Check to see if it matches the logo on the site you were looking at.

7

HOW CAN YOU TELL IF A NEWS STORY ON SOCIAL MEDIA IS RELIABLE?

a. It contains a lot of detail and includes a photo.

b. It comes from a trustworthy news organization.

c. It was the first one to come up in a search, so that means it's likely the most accurate.

8

"STRANGE RAIN: WHY FISH, FROGS, AND GOLF BALLS FALL FROM THE SKIES." THIS INCREDIBLE HEADLINE ACTUALLY APPEARED IN *SMITHSONIAN* MAGAZINE IN 2015. HOW WOULD YOU CHECK IF THIS STORY IS REAL OR FAKE?

a. Do an internet search on the topic to see if there are other similar stories.

b. Consider the source of the information. Go to Smithsonian.com and find out what the publication is all about.

c. Do a search on the experts quoted in the story. Do they come from legitimate organizations?

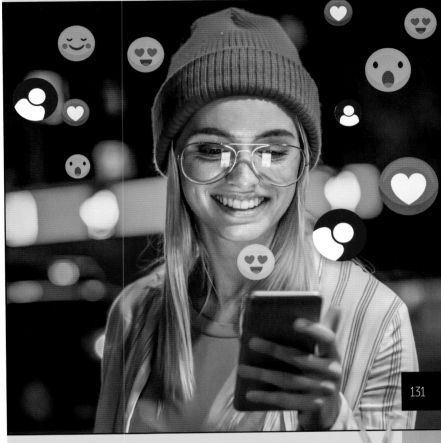

131

As social media usage increases, a rising number of influencers use their posts to share their ideas and to sway people's opinions.

ANSWERS

1. C. SOMETIMES HEADLINES ARE MISLEADING. MAYBE SOMEONE PLAYED A JOKE ON THE CAFETERIA LADY BY PLANTING FAKE RATS IN THE LETTUCE BIN. THAT'S TOTALLY WORTH SHARING, TOO, BUT IT'S A COMPLETELY DIFFERENT STORY FROM WHAT THE HEADLINE LED YOU TO BELIEVE.

2. B. NEVER CLICK ON SOMETHING THAT OFFERS YOU A FREE PRIZE OR LOCKS YOUR SCREEN, AND DEFINITELY DO NOT ENTER ANY PERSONAL INFORMATION ON THE INTERNET WITHOUT ASKING YOUR PARENTS FIRST. PEOPLE WITH BAD INTENTIONS SOMETIMES TRY TO COLLECT INFORMATION THIS WAY.

3. C. THE BEST WAY TO LIMIT THE SPREAD OF FALSE STORIES IS TO SHARE THE CORRECTION THE SAME WAY YOU SHARED THE ORIGINAL STORY.

4. A AND C. SOMETIMES PHOTO FAKES ARE SO GOOD THAT THEY LOOK COMPLETELY REAL.

5. B. PRANKSTERS SOMETIMES TRY TO CREATE FAKE SOCIAL MEDIA ACCOUNTS FOR FAMOUS PEOPLE.

6. ALL OF THE ABOVE. THESE ARE ALL GREAT WAYS TO DETECT A FAKE WEBSITE.

7. B. IF THE INFORMATION COMES FROM A GOOD SOURCE, THAT'S A SIGN THAT IT'S RELIABLE. AND READING ABOUT THE SAME TOPIC ON MORE THAN ONE NEWS SITE IS ALWAYS A GOOD IDEA TO PROTECT AGAINST BIAS.

8. ALL OF THE ABOVE. BELIEVE IT OR NOT, THIS STORY IS TRUE. SCIENTISTS BELIEVE THAT, IN RARE CASES, TORNADOES OR WATERSPOUTS SUCK UP SMALL ANIMALS OR GOLF BALLS FROM THE LAND AND THEN DROP THEM IN ANOTHER LOCATION. FOR THE FULL STORY, GO TO SMITHSONIAN.COM AND SEARCH "RAINING FROGS."

TRAFFIC JAM ON EVEREST

132

Who would believe that the top of the world's tallest mountain could be as busy as a city street? But that was exactly the case on a sunny day in May 2019, when climber Nirmal Purja took this photograph. Some 250 to 300 people were marching single-file toward the summit—along the edge of a dangerous cliff. Some climbers were delayed for as long as three hours.

Mount Everest isn't this busy every day. The climbers all came out at once because of the good weather. But overcrowding on the mountain has become a big problem. It's a threat to the climbers, who are exposed to freezing temperatures and high altitudes for longer periods of time. Plus, the crowds have been leaving behind tons of trash.

Purja's incredible photo went viral and called attention to the environmental damage and dangers caused by tourists trekking to the rooftop of the world.

Media companies are always looking for innovative ways to use technology to present complicated data and deliver the news.

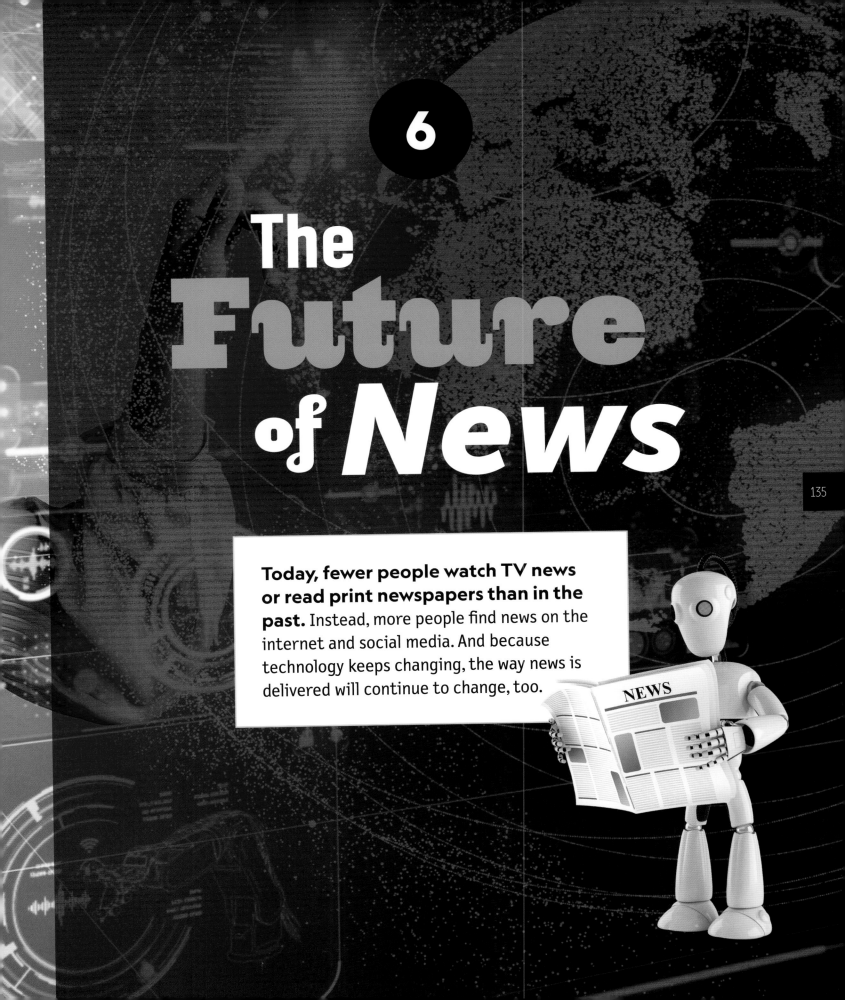

The Future of News

6

Today, fewer people watch TV news or read print newspapers than in the past. Instead, more people find news on the internet and social media. And because technology keeps changing, the way news is delivered will continue to change, too.

7 WAYS NEWS WILL Change

Technology has transformed the news throughout its history. In the past, these sudden changes have led to chaotic periods filled with a lot of false information—just like today. The printing press in the 1400s led to centuries of news pamphlets and early newspapers that spouted gossip, propaganda, news, and everything in between.

In the early 1900s, printing presses became so speedy that publishers could print hundreds of thousands of newspapers at once and sell them for a penny each. "Yellow journalism" exploded in popularity, with wild headlines that attracted huge numbers of readers. Those headlines were the "clickbait" of the time. Eventually, yellow journalism faded away in part because the public became more interested in news from reliable newspapers.

Now, the internet has become the new penny press, where strong journalism lives alongside clickbait. And everyone is trying to figure out how to tame this digital Wild West.

Technology is changing so fast that no one knows for sure what news will look like in 10 years. Read on for seven of the cutting-edge changes—happening right now—that are likely to determine our future.

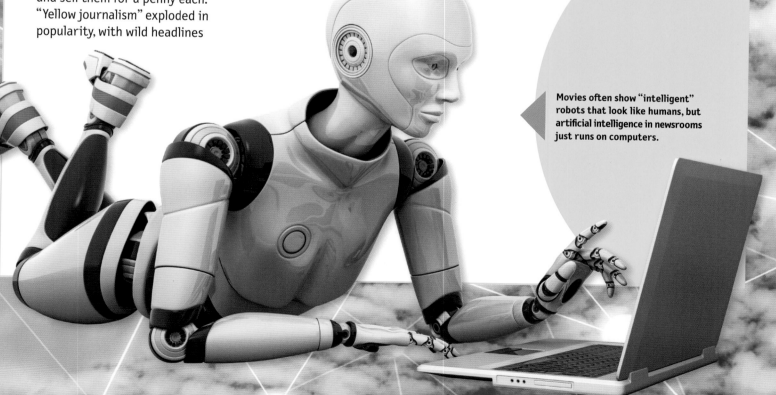

Movies often show "intelligent" robots that look like humans, but artificial intelligence in newsrooms just runs on computers.

1 MACHINES WILL Write EVEN MORE NEWS.

Some of the biggest news organizations, including the *New York Times* and *Washington Post,* already use computers to find news stories, pull in facts for articles, and write some headlines. The *Post* has used computer software to gather information and report stories on high school sports, elections, and even the Olympics. Most articles at the *Post* and other news organizations are still written by human beings, but the technology is getting "smarter" all the time.

In the future, news organizations may also use apps or software to translate news stories into different languages. Right now, the technology is still pretty clunky. It has trouble telling the difference between words that have more than one meaning, such as "a rock band," or "an elastic hair band." Translating expressions, such as "hold your horses" or "when pigs fly," is also a challenge for machines. You can imagine how hilarious it would be if a computer translated these sayings word for word. For now, human translators often do a better job than machines at understanding the meaning of words, but the computer programs are catching up quickly.

Machine translation of news would open up a world of new information, as people could read stories from around the globe that are not currently translated. But if a machine were to make a mistake, it could have serious consequences. What if a statement by a world leader is bungled in translation and offends other countries? Or what if translation technology messes up emergency messages during a natural disaster?

Fear not. These machines won't completely replace people anytime soon. Human journalists will always need to investigate and uncover stories that computers cannot find. And translation technology has a ways to go before it could completely replace human translators. But machine-made news will surely increase in the years to come.

2 MOBILE WILL Rule.

In 2018, several major news organizations reported that 50 percent of their audience reads their stories on mobile devices, and that number jumps to 80 percent for news on Twitter. In the future, even more people will opt for on-the-go news on their smartphones, smart watches, and other mobile devices.

Daily news stories will likely get even shorter to make them easier to read on smartphones. But longer stories will be available for people who want a more in-depth read. Photos, graphics, podcasts, and videos will continue to be popular, and will become even easier to use on mobile devices.

It's fun to think that news will become even more interactive, and that you'll be able to read and watch it in so many different forms. But shorter stories can also make complicated topics seem simpler than they are. Many readers then may not look for the more in-depth stories. Also, when headlines and images are paired with shorter text, they have a much greater influence on readers' opinions—so they need to be accurate.

THERE ARE MORE MOBILE PHONES ON EARTH THAN PEOPLE.

3 LOCAL NEWS COULD MAKE A Comeback.

Local newspapers are becoming extinct because advertisers and readers have shifted to online news. But people still want to know what's happening in their community. Some social media sites and nonprofit organizations are beginning to step in to meet this need, providing local stories to people in smaller cities and towns.

Some communities will be able to get news about local sports teams and elections through their social media accounts. But others will not. Social media sites do not create original content, they just pull in news from other sources. And in March 2019, Facebook announced that one out of three users lives in places where the company could not find enough local news content to distribute through its app. So local news will not make a full rebound until companies start paying journalists to write more local stories.

> **?** What would you like to know from your local news?

ABOUT 21 PERCENT OF AMERICANS NOW GET NEWS ON YOUTUBE.

4 TV NEWS WILL Converge WITH INTERNET NEWS.

Adults over 50 are two times more likely than younger adults to get a lot of news from television. And younger adults are twice as likely to get a lot of news online. So future generations will likely continue to shift toward online news. In 10 years, it's possible that almost everyone will watch "television news" on the internet, and many will do so on mobile devices.

This means news will change completely. More news events are already being live-streamed. And much of our video news will probably come from social media sites and video-on-demand services. Companies such as Amazon and Netflix have bigger international audiences than traditional TV news networks do. These specific companies don't currently have plans to get into the news business, but it's possible that companies like them may one day offer news to people all over the globe.

And what will video news even look like? Will people still want to watch traditional newscasters sitting behind desks if they are watching on mobile devices? As technology keeps improving, we may get news in ways we cannot even imagine today.

138

In the future, smart glasses may put computer-generated information directly into a user's line of sight or ears.

5 YOU'LL BE ABLE TO **Wear** YOUR NEWS.

Smart watches, like the Apple Watch, are just the beginning of wearable technology. In the future, you may read the news on special glasses, gloves, or even on your pants!

These devices will be attached to your body and will travel with you everywhere you go. This means you will no longer need a pocket big enough to hold your smartphone, and it's probably less likely you'll drop it and smash the screen.

These mobile devices can be helpful, but they can also collect a lot of personal information about your interests, age, and health, as well as where you live and the places you go every day. That might not seem like a big deal, but what if that information fell into the wrong hands?

In 2017, soldiers in a war zone in Syria accidentally revealed the position of secret U.S. military locations because they were wearing fitness tracking devices. The soldiers had failed to disable the GPS trackers in the devices, which shared their location through the app.

Even for regular people, sharing all of this information has risks. As you read the news on your wearable device, the company that sold you the device may track what you are reading, who you are sharing information with, what you are clicking on and buying online, and much more. It can then sell that personal information to other companies without your knowledge.

And what if hackers access your account? They would know exactly where you are all day, every day, and what time you go to sleep, which could make it easier for them to target you or your property for a crime. If you leave your wearable somewhere, a savvy thief could use it to access all the other devices to which it's connected, such as your phone or computer.

In the future, governments could start regulating these devices to better protect customers, but right now, security experts say companies need to do a lot more to keep personal information safe.

With the right app, a smart watch gives you access to news on the go, simply by looking at your wrist.

6 NEWS WILL BE **PERSONALIZED** AND LOCATION-BASED.

Social media apps will continue to feed you information they know you like and go further to customize individual stories just for you. For example, your news about a local election might include results for your district, while a friend in the next town over might see something different. Or if you're riding past the local sports arena in a car, and your hometown team just scored a huge victory, the awesome news might pop up on your phone just because you were in the neighborhood.

The coolest part about this is that the news comes to you. Your mobile device "knows" what you want and gives it to you. But you will face the same privacy concerns as you do with wearable devices. And you may not be exposed to stories about ideas, issues, problems, or people you didn't even know you wanted to learn about. You'll have to decide if you think the personalized news is worth the risk.

THE BATTLE AGAINST **Bogus** NEWS WILL CONTINUE.

7 Technology companies are working to weed out false news stories with artificial intelligence (AI), or computer software that "learns" as it goes along. In many ways, these computer programs act like human fact-checkers—except they work at lightning speed. The computers look for telltale signs of false stories: headlines written in all capital letters or that have tons of misspellings; overuse of adjectives and adverbs—a sign that the story may be sensational; or a lack of quotes, which suggests it's missing reliable sources. They also compare articles with other similar stories on the internet.

One company claimed that its program caught 90 percent of the false stories it reviewed and could even separate funny satire from harmful hoaxes. But there is one thing these machines cannot do yet. They don't understand the meaning of words, so incorrect information, such as "An orange is not a fruit," can easily escape notice.

AI improves by leaps and bounds every year, but so does the technology that helps people make fake content. In the near future, it will be possible for computer programs to create speech that sounds exactly like the voice of a specific person, allowing fakers to string together entire conversations that never really happened. And software already exists that makes it possible to alter voice recordings, allowing an editor to move words around and change which words the speaker emphasizes. Machines are also getting better at creating false videos and images that look completely real.

This sounds cool, but imagine the consequences. Someone could create a fake audio or video of a world leader making an offensive statement, even if the leader never actually said it. What if the false comments are so terrible that they turn citizens against the leader or cause a conflict with another country? Or what if the same thing happened to someone in your school, and everyone got angry at the person over a statement he or she never made? AI that detects false content will be in an endless race against the people who create fake stories—each trying to outdo the other with newer and better technology. So everyone will have to be even more careful about what to believe on the internet and social media.

You can get all the news that's fit to print (or post) just for you with a personalized news app.

141

WHAT'S Next?

I n the future, people will continue to "break news" on mobile devices or computers and distribute it to millions of others in seconds. And it will be even trickier to figure out which information to believe.

That's why you—yes, you—need to be media literate. That means understanding the different kinds of media—from TV and print to social media, videos, text messages, and more—and thinking about who created each piece of information and why. Part of media literacy is also knowing how to spot misinformation and avoid spreading it to others so that you stay safe and that information doesn't harm others.

Having the tools to recognize reliable journalism is important. Trustworthy journalists will continue to act as our watchdogs, keeping an eye out for wrongdoing and corruption. Whether their work appears in a paper or on a wristwatch, it will help keep our society free.

MAJOR EVENTS IN News History

59 B.C.
At Julius Caesar's command, the *Acta diurna*, which includes daily news, is posted in public places. It's the earliest known forerunner of the newspaper. **PAGE 16**

A.D. 618
A newsletter called the *bao* is printed in China using wooden blocks. The newsletter is only distributed to rulers and other high-level officials. **PAGE 17**

About 1450
German craftsman Johannes Gutenberg patents his printing press. **PAGE 17**

1566
Weekly handwritten newsletters, called *gazzette* or *avvisi*, are sold in Venice, Italy.

1620
The first newspapers in English and French are printed in Amsterdam—Europe's publishing hub at the time.

1670
A letter in England shows the first-known use of the term "newes paper."

1690
The first newspaper is printed in the American colonies. **PAGE 18**

1722
The first newspaper in Latin America, *La Gaceta de México (Gazette of Mexico)*, launches in Mexico City.

1783
The *Pennsylvania Evening Post* becomes America's first daily paper.

1791
The First Amendment to the U.S. Constitution guarantees freedom of the press.

1808
The first U.S. Spanish-language newspaper, *El Misisipí*, publishes in New Orleans, Louisiana. **PAGE 51**

1814
A newspaper is printed on a press powered by a steam engine that could print 5,000 copies per hour. **PAGE 20**

1827
Freedom's Journal is the first African-American newspaper printed in the United States. **PAGE 52**

1828
The *Cherokee Phoenix* becomes the first Native American newspaper, printed in both English and the Cherokee language. **PAGE 51**

1833
The *New York Sun* is the first successful "penny paper" in the United States. **PAGE 20**

1844
Richard Hoe patents an improved printing press than can churn out more than 8,000 copies an hour.

1860
The fastest way to get news from the midwestern United States to California is by Pony Express—messengers on horseback.

1861
The first telegraph line to San Francisco puts the Pony Express out of business.

1868
The typewriter is invented.

1876
Alexander Graham Bell patents the telephone. **PAGE 20**

1897
The first color funnies appear in the *New York Journal*.

1903
The *Daily Mirror* in London becomes the first "tabloid" newspaper.

142

1906
Canadian Reginald Fessenden uses radio waves to transmit voice and music.

1919
The first scheduled radio broadcast airs in the Netherlands.

1920–21
About 30 radio stations go on the air in the United States. **PAGE 23**

1930s
The facsimile telegraph allows newspapers to send photographs over telephone and telegraph lines.

1933
Franklin D. Roosevelt is the first U.S. president to use radio to communicate with the public, with "fireside chats."

1941
Eighteen U.S. television stations get approval from the government to begin broadcasting. CBS and NBC in New York are the first to air.

1941
The first paid TV commercial airs.

1946
One of the first Spanish-language radio stations in the United States, KCOR-AM, is founded in San Antonio, Texas.

1952
The term "anchor" is used to describe the person presenting the news on TV.

1960
Vice President Richard M. Nixon and Senator John F. Kennedy face off in the first televised presidential debate. **PAGE 29**

1972–74
Reporters Bob Woodward and Carl Bernstein report on the Watergate scandal. **PAGE 30**

1980
CNN launches as the first 24-hour TV news channel. **PAGE 26**

1982
USA Today is published. It's the first national newspaper to print in color.

1991
The general public begins to use the World Wide Web.

1995
Media organizations start reporting news on the internet.

2004
The social media network Facebook is born. **PAGE 117**

2005
YouTube begins operating, making it easy for people to post videos online.

2006
Twitter's co-founder Jack Dorsey posts the first tweet.

2007
The first hashtag appears on Twitter.

2015
Snapchat introduces the "Discover" feature, which includes news stories. **PAGE 119**

2017
Collins English Dictionary names "fake news" as word of the year, defined as "false, often sensational, information disseminated under the guise of news reporting."

2018
Instagram reaches a billion users.

2019
More than half of U.S. adults get news from social media.

MEET THE EXPERTS

A number of accomplished journalists and media experts reviewed and contributed to this project. Our panelists hail from some of the most prestigious media organizations in the country and include winners of some of the top awards in journalism.

NAFTALI BENDAVID is currently the deputy campaign editor for the *Washington Post* and has worked for the *Wall Street Journal, Chicago Tribune,* and *Miami Herald,* among other news organizations. He has covered the White House, Justice Department, and Congress. From 2013 through 2015, he was stationed in Brussels, Belgium, reporting on the European Union, NATO, and European social issues for the *Journal.* Bendavid covered Al Gore's 2000 U.S. presidential campaign and the subsequent election recount, and he wrote *The Thumpin',* a book about the 2006 U.S. congressional election. He has appeared on CNN's *Inside Politics, The Colbert Report,* and various National Public Radio news programs.

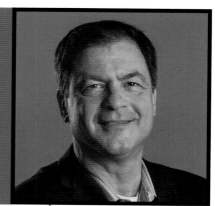

> " I love talking to **interesting** people I'd otherwise never meet, figuring out **fascinating** things that are happening, and crafting **colorful** or compelling articles." —NAFTALI BENDAVID

MARCIA BULLARD is the retired president and CEO of *USA Weekend,* the national magazine formerly distributed in 600 U.S. newspapers. She was a founding editor of *USA Today* and has 36 years of experience as a CEO, publisher, editor, and reporter in national and local media.

As an executive with Gannett Co. Inc., Bullard twice received its top award, the President's Ring. She was honored with the 2013 Business Gives Back Award at George Washington University (GWU) and the President's Volunteer Service Award in 2005, and was named Revlon Business Woman of the Year in 1998.

In 1992, Bullard founded Make a Difference Day—the nation's largest day of volunteering. She serves on several nonprofit boards, including as board president of the Fund for Investigative Journalism.

She started in the news business at age 17 in Springfield, Illinois, earned a B.S. in journalism from Southern Illinois University and an M.B.A. from GWU in Washington, D.C. Bullard taught journalism at the University of Rochester in New York. She resides in Washington, D.C., and Philadelphia, Pennsylvania, where her husband retired as an editor at the *Philadelphia Inquirer.*

LYDIA CHÁVEZ graduated from the University of California (UC), Berkeley, with a B.A. in comparative literature and the Columbia School of Journalism with an M.A. in journalism before she took her first job with her hometown paper, the *Albuquerque Tribune.* She worked as a researcher at *Esquire* magazine and *Time* magazine and as a reporter with the *Los Angeles Times* and the *New York Times,* covering business and then the war in El Salvador and the return of democracy in Argentina. She taught for nearly three decades at the Graduate School of Journalism at UC Berkeley, and today she runs Mission Local, an online news lab in San Francisco.

MICHAEL H. COTTMAN is an award-winning journalist, author, and former political reporter for the *Washington Post.* Today, he edits and reports for the NBCBLK section of NBC News Digital. His past books include *Shackles From the Deep,* which traces the path of a sunken slave ship. The book earned a starred review from *Booklist* and was selected as a Notable Social Studies Trade Book by the Children's Book Council in 2018. He is also the author of *The Wreck of the Henrietta Marie* and *Million Man March.* He has appeared on National Public Radio's *Tell Me More,* CNN, History channel, and *The Oprah Winfrey Show* to discuss his work. Cottman, who has received numerous awards, was also part of a reporting team that won journalism's highest honor, the Pulitzer Prize, for *Newsday*'s coverage of a deadly subway crash in New York in 1992. He lives in Silver Spring, Maryland, and when he's not reporting, he's spending time with his daughter, Ariane.

SUSAN GOLDBERG is editorial director of National Geographic Partners and editor in chief of *National Geographic* magazine. Under her leadership, *National Geographic* has been honored with five National Magazine Awards, including the top prize for General Excellence, and was a finalist for the Pulitzer Prize for Feature Photography and for Explanatory Reporting. Goldberg also has led reporting that was honored with multiple awards, including the Pulitzer Prize in San Jose, and a finalist for the Pulitzer at the (Cleveland) *Plain Dealer.* Before her work at *National Geographic,* Goldberg ran Bloomberg News' Washington Bureau, was the top editor at the *Mercury News* and *Plain Dealer,* and served in editing or reporting jobs at *USA Today,* the *Detroit Free Press,* and the *Seattle Post-Intelligencer.*

CLARK HOYT is a Pulitzer Prize–winning journalist and retired ombudsman for the *New York Times,* where his job was to ensure the newspaper adhered to the highest standards of journalism. Hoyt also served as a director of the American Society of Newspaper Editors Foundation and was the former chair of the National Press Foundation.

Before joining the *Times,* Hoyt spent much of his career with the Knight Ridder newspaper company, where he served as vice president of news and later oversaw the news organization's Washington, D.C., bureau. In 1973, Hoyt earned a Pulitzer Prize, along with his colleague Robert S. Boyd, for their coverage of vice presidential nominee Thomas Eagleton's struggles with severe depression. In 2004, Hoyt received the John S. Knight Gold Medal, the highest employee award Knight Ridder confers.

ANNA KASSINGER is the former director of curriculum for Newseum Education at the Newseum in Washington, D.C. She led the creation of face-to-face and virtual classes for students in elementary school through college; professional development workshops for educators; and content for the Newseum's award-winning platform, *NewseumED.org.* Previously, Kassinger co-founded ARTLAB+, the Smithsonian's first digital media studio for teens. She earned a B.A. from Pomona College in Claremont, California, and an Ed.M. from Harvard Graduate School of Education in Cambridge, Massachusetts. Her work has been recognized by the National Council for the Social Studies, the American Association of School Librarians, and the Association for Education in Journalism and Mass Communications.

" *I think we'll see two* **trends** *in the coming years: more visual* **storytelling** *and a greater appreciation for* **local news** *producers. I see a hunger from 'readers' to* **see** *and* **hear** *and even experience what reporters see and hear in the* **field** *... I expect that as the* **technology** *becomes cheaper, more news reports will be built to make us feel like we are actually in places and part of* **events** *far from home.*" —ANNA KASSINGER

LINDA KAUSS earned a journalism degree from Arizona State University and has worked as a reporter and editor for the *Phoenix Gazette,* the *Pacific Daily News* in Guam, and the *Florida Times-Union* in Jacksonville.

In 1983, she joined the staff of the newly launched national newspaper *USA Today,* where she spent the next 32 years supervising the reporting teams covering medicine, science, psychology, education, and later, the White House, Justice Department, and U.S. Supreme Court. She retired in 2015, and lives in Great Falls, Virginia, with her husband, Clark Hoyt.

BRENT KENDALL is a Washington, D.C.–based legal affairs reporter for the *Wall Street Journal.* He covers the U.S. Supreme Court and lower federal courts around the country. He has been a journalist in the nation's capital since 2002. Kendall's previous stops include Dow Jones Newswires, the Los Angeles *Daily Journal,* and the *Washington Monthly.* He is a graduate of the University of North Carolina at Chapel Hill and American University in Washington, D.C.

ANN E. MARIMOW covers legal affairs for the *Washington Post*, where she has worked since 2005. She previously covered state government and politics at the *Concord Monitor* in New Hampshire, for the San Jose *Mercury News* in California, and for the *Post* in Maryland. She grew up in Philadelphia in a newspaper family and graduated from Cornell University in Ithaca, New York, where she covered sports for the *Cornell Daily Sun.* In 2015, Marimow was a Nieman Journalism Fellow at Harvard University, where she studied law and poetry.

TREVY A. MCDONALD is an associate professor of broadcast and electronic journalism at the University of North Carolina at Chapel Hill. She received her B.A. in radio/TV/film from the University of Wisconsin–Oshkosh, her M.A. in radio, television, and motion pictures and a Ph.D. in journalism and mass communication, both from the University of North Carolina at Chapel Hill. She teaches courses in electronic communication and diversity and media. Her research interests include media socialization, audience studies, oral history, and race and gender.

McDonald is the co-editor of two scholarly anthologies: *Nature of a Sistuh: Black Women's Lived Experiences in Contemporary Culture* and *Building Diverse Communities: Applications of Communication Research.* She is also the author of the novels *Time Will Tell* and *Round 'Bout Midnight,* and has contributed to numerous anthologies and publications.

She is currently writing a series of chapter books about the U.S. civil rights movement for middle-grade readers.

> **"** *Journalists serve as* **eyewitnesses** *to history. They* **document** *what becomes history as it is occurring."* —TREVY A. MCDONALD

ROBIN SPROUL spent 41 years at ABC News, including 22 years as Washington bureau chief. She is the recipient of many journalism awards, including Emmy, duPont-Columbia, Peabody, and Ohio State awards. She served as ABC's liaison to the federal government; oversaw political debates and interviews, including the program *This Week With George Stephanopoulos*; and managed ABC's polling operations. In 2018, she received the Lifetime Achievement Award from the Washington Press Club Foundation. In 2015, she was named one of the "100 Most Influential People in Washington" and one of *Washingtonian* magazine's "Most Powerful Women," and she was awarded the First Amendment Service Award by the Radio Television Digital News Association. She is a past chair of the board of the National Press Foundation and currently serves on the board of the Shorenstein Center at Harvard Kennedy School.

Glossary

ANCHORPERSON: A broadcaster on a television news program who delivers the news and introduces reports by other journalists.

BIAS: Favoritism to some ideas or facts over others.

BREAKING NEWS: New reports about an event that happened the same day or sometimes a day earlier. These stories often answer the questions who, what, where, when, and why.

CENSORSHIP: The blocking of news stories, books, movies, or other information from being published.

CLICKBAIT: Sensational headlines on websites and social media designed to get you to click; often takes you to a page with no article or to an article that doesn't live up to the headline.

CONSPIRACY THEORY: A false belief that powerful people have secretly plotted to hide certain information or are behind a particular event.

COPYRIGHT: The legal right to publish, sell, or reproduce works such as news stories, books, movies, and songs, among other materials.

CORRECTION: A written statement by a news organization that corrects a mistake in an earlier article.

DEFAMATION: A false statement that harms a person's reputation or ability to work.

DISINFORMATION: False information deliberately spread to affect public opinion or hide the truth.

FALSE NEWS: Entirely or partially false information spread either to mislead people and influence their opinions or to make a profit by generating a lot of clicks (and advertising dollars).

FIGHTING WORDS: Statements that could cause other people to commit illegal or violent acts, or that could cause direct harm to others.

GIF: Short online video.

GO VIRAL: The rapid spread of videos, photos, or other information on social media.

HOAX: A false story intended to trick people; can be a joke or a harmful negative story intended to spread disinformation.

HUMAN-INTEREST STORY: A story about people that appeals to readers' or viewers' emotions.

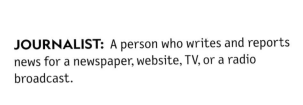

JOURNALIST: A person who writes and reports news for a newspaper, website, TV, or a radio broadcast.

LIBEL: A defamatory statement (*see* defamation) made in writing, pictures, or any other physical form.

MISINFORMATION: The spread of false information, with or without the intention to mislead others.

NEWS: Information that aims to inform the public by providing accurate facts about what is happening in the world. News strives for balance and includes different points of view in each story. News can be shared through television, radio, websites, social media, newspapers, and other sources.

OPINION PIECE: An article or TV or radio segment (or show) that presents one person's views about a topic, often including facts that support only one side of an issue.

PLAGIARISM: Publishing someone else's text, photographs, videos, or any other copyrighted material without permission or giving credit to the original source.

PROPAGANDA: Messages that aim to change people's ideas and actions to benefit a specific cause or organization, often using false information to mislead people or hide the truth.

REPORTER: A person whose job is to gather and report the news.

RETRACTION: A statement by a newspaper that an earlier story was incorrect.

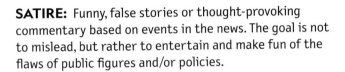

SATIRE: Funny, false stories or thought-provoking commentary based on events in the news. The goal is not to mislead, but rather to entertain and make fun of the flaws of public figures and/or policies.

SLANDER: A defamatory statement (*see* defamation) that is spoken. This applies to TV and radio news as well as videos, podcasts, and even speeches.

SOCIAL MEDIA: Online communities and apps that allow users to share messages and information with each other.

SPONSORED CONTENT: Promotional content or advertisements made to look like regular articles or social media posts

TABLOID: A website or newspaper—often about half the size of a traditional newspaper—that features sensational stories of celebrity gossip, crime, and scandals.

TRANSPARENCY: A professional standard that requires journalists to be open and honest about where information comes from, how they know what they know, and whether any personal or business relationships could influence the way a story is reported.

Sources for Pop-up Facts

INTRODUCTION

(p.10, kids and teens) Robb, M. B. "News and America's Kids: How Young People Perceive and Are Impacted by the News." Common Sense. 2017, commonsensemedia.org/sites/default/files/uploads/research/2017_commonsense_newsandamericaskids.pdf.

CHAPTER 2

(p. 41, China) ifex.org. "China: Riddles and Funny Memes Outwit Online Censors." 2018, ifex.org/china-riddles-and-funny-memes-outwit-online-censors.

CHAPTER 3

(p. 61, WWI) Cook, Ian. "World War One: Propaganda as a Weapon? Influencing International Opinion." British Library, 2014, bl.uk/world-war-one/articles/propaganda-as-a-weapon.

(p. 69, Facebook) "Russia-backed Facebook Posts 'Reached 126m Americans' During US Election." *The Guardian*, October 30, 2017, theguardian.com/technology/2017/oct/30/facebook-russia-fake-accounts-126-million.

CHAPTER 4

(p. 95, social media) Shearer, Elisa, and Jeffrey Gottfried. "News Use Across Social Media Platforms." Pew Research Center, 2017, journalism.org/2017/09/07/news-use-across-social-media-platforms-2017.

(p. 96, poll) Jones, Jeffrey M., and Zacc Ritter. "Americans See More News Bias; Most Can't Name Neutral Source." Gallup/Knight Foundation, 2017, news.gallup.com/poll/225755/americans-news-bias-name-neutral-source.aspx.

(p. 103, opinion as fact) Mitchell, Amy, and others. "Distinguishing Between Factual and Opinion Statements in the News." Pew Research Center, 2018, journalism.org/2018/06/18/republicans-and-democrats-more-likely-to-classify-a-news-statement-as-factual-if-it-favors-their-side-whether-it-is-factual-or-opinion.

(p. 110, Facebook) Reiff, Nathan. "Top Companies Owned by Facebook." Investopedia, June 15, 2019, investopedia.com/articles/personal-finance/051815/top-11-companies-owned-facebook.asp.

CHAPTER 5

(p. 116, poll) Robb. "News and America's Kids."

(p. 119, clickbait) Chakraborty, Abhijnan, and others. "Tabloids in the Era of Social Media?: Understanding the Production and Consumption of Clickbaits in Twitter." Journal Proceedings of the ACM on Human-Computer Interaction 1, CSCW, November 2017: article no. 30: 3, doi.org/10.1145/3134665.

(p. 121, Twitter) Vosoughi, S., Deb Roy, and Sinan Aral. "The Spread of True and False News Online." Science 359, no. 6380 (March 9, 2018): 1146–1151, doi.org/10.1126/science.aap9559.

(p. 123, sharing false news) Robb. "News and America's Kids."

CHAPTER 6

(p. 137, mobile phones) Harden, James. "Future of News." BBC, 2015, bbc.co.uk/news/resources/idt-bbb9e158-4a1b-43c7-8b3b-9651938d4d6a.

(p. 138, YouTube) Shearer and Gottfried. "News Use Across Social Media Platforms."

Further Resources

For Tweens & Teens

Play fun games and show off your social media smarts:
digitalcompass.org/game/index.html

Get fact-checking tools: **commonsensemedia.org/lists/
fact-checking-tools-for-teens-and-tweens**

Learn more about the rules that good journalists follow
from the Society of Professional Journalists:
spj.org/ethicscode.asp

Get news just for kids at these websites:

Smithsonian Tween Tribune
tweentribune.com

Dogo News
dogonews.com

News For Kids
newsforkids.net

For Parents and Teachers

These media literacy websites offer helpful tools for
parents and lesson plans for teachers:

American Library Association's Literacy Clearinghouse
literacy.ala.org/897-2

Common Sense Media
commonsensemedia.org

Media Literacy Clearinghouse
frankwbaker.com/mlc

News Literacy Project
newslit.org

Bibliography

Abernathy, Penelope M. *The Rise of a New Media Baron and the Emerging Threat of News Deserts*. University of North Carolina Press, 2016. newspaperownership .com/executive-summary.

Allen, Louise C., Ernest A. Sharpe, and John R. Whitaker. "Newspapers." In Handbook of Texas Online. Texas State Historical Society. tshaonline.org/handbook/online/ articles/een08.

American Press Institute. "Journalism Essentials." Accessed January 20, 2018. americanpressinstitute.org/journalism-essentials.

Anderson, C. W., Leonard Downie, Jr., and Michael Schudson. *The News Media: What Everyone Needs to Know*. New York: Oxford University Press, 2016.

Barthel, Michael, Amy Mitchell, and Jesse Holcomb. "Many Americans Believe Fake News Is Sowing Confusion." Pew Research Center, 2016. www.journalism.org/ 2016/12/15/many-americans-believe-fake-news-is-sowing-confusion.

Brown, Rob. *Public Relations and the Social Web: How to Use Social Media and Web 2.0 in Communications*. London: Kogan Page Limited, 2009.

Chakraborty, Abhijnan, and others. "Tabloids in the Era of Social Media?: Understanding the Production and Consumption of Clickbaits in Twitter." *Journal Proceedings of the ACM on Human-Computer Interaction 1*, Issue CSCW, November 2017: Article no. 30. doi.org/10.1145/3134665.

Chandrasekhar, C. P. "The Business of News in the Age of the Internet." *Social Scientist* 41, no. 5/6 (May/June 2013): 25–39.

Collomb, Jean-Daniel. "The Ideology of Climate Change Denial in the United States." *European Journal of American Studies* 9, no. 1 (spring 2014). document 5. doi.org/ 10.4000/ejas.10305.

Colson, V. "Science Blogs as Competing Channels for the Dissemination of Science News." *Journalism* 12, no. 7 (September 2011): 889–902. doi.org/10.1177/ 1464884911412834.

De Hamel, Christopher. *Scribes and Illuminators* (Medieval Craftsman series). University of Toronto Press, 1992.

Dixon, Travis L., and Charlotte L. Williams. "The Changing Misrepresentation of Race and Crime on Network and Cable News." *Journal of Communication* 65, no. 1 (February 2015): 24–39. doi.org/10.1111/jcom.12133.

Grady, Cheryl L., Anthony R. McIntosh, M. Natasha Rajah, and Fergus I. M. Craik. "Neural Correlates of the Episodic Encoding of Pictures and Words." *Proceedings of the National Academy of Sciences* 95, no. 5 (March 1998): 2703–08. doi.org/10.1073/ pnas.95.5.2703.

Hutton, Frankie, and Barbara Straus Reed, eds. *Outsiders in the 19th-Century Press History: Multicultural Perspectives*. Bowling Green State University Popular Press, 1995.

Hindman, Matthew, and Vlad Barash. "Disinformation, 'Fake News' and Influence Campaigns on Twitter." Knight Foundation, 2018. knightfoundation.org/reports/ disinformation-fake-news-and-influence-campaigns-on-twitter.

Josepher, Bryce. "Political Media Bias in the United States: Immigration and the Trump Administration." Master's thesis, 2017. University of South Florida. scholarcommons.usf.edu/etd/7041.

Jowett, Garth S., and Victoria O'Donnell. *Propaganda & Persuasion*, 5th ed. Los Angeles: SAGE, 2012.

Kroll, Luisa, and Kerry A. Dolan, eds. "Forbes 400: The Definitive Ranking of the Wealthiest Americans." *Forbes*, October 3, 2018. forbes.com/forbes-400/ #1f114f5f7e2f.

Mansfield, Matt, and Ellen Shearer, eds. *Truth Counts: A Practical Guide for News Consumers*. Washington, D.C.: CQ, 2018.

Mitchell, Amy, and others. "Distinguishing Between Factual and Opinion Statements in the News." Pew Research Center, 2018. journalism.org/2018/06/18/ distinguishing-between-factual-and-opinion-statements-in-the-news.

Mitchell, Amy, and others. "Political Polarization and Media Habits." Pew Research Center, 2014. journalism.org/2014/10/21/political-polarization-media-habits.

Pelda, Kurt. "Separating Facts From Fiction in Conflict Reporting." In *Conflict Reporting in the Smartphone Era: From Budget Constraints to Information Warfare*, ed. by Darija FabijaniÐ, Christian Spahr, and Vladimir Zlatarsky. Konrad-Adenauer-Stiftung, 2016. kas.de/c/document_library/get_file?uuid=82b41c40-fd3a-3321-6196-f80720a6696e&groupId=252038.

Pettegree, Andrew. *The Invention of News: How the World Came to Know About Itself*. Yale University Press, 2014.

Porter, Jeff. *Lost Sound: The Forgotten Art of Radio Storytelling*. University of North Carolina Press, 2016.

Robb, M. B. "News and America's Kids: How Young People Perceive and Are Impacted by the News." San Francisco, CA: Common Sense, 2017. commonsensemedia.org/sites/ default/files/uploads/research/2017_commonsense_newsandamericaskids.pdf.

Roberts, Gene, and Hank Klibanoff. *The Race Beat: The Press, the Civil Rights Struggle, and the Awakening of a Nation*. New York: Vintage Books, 2006.

Shearer, Elisa, and Jeffrey Gottfried. "News Use Across Social Media Platforms 2017." Pew Research Center, 2017. journalism.org/2017/09/07/news-use-across-social-media-platforms-2017.

Stephens, Mitchell. *A History of News*, 3rd ed. New York: Oxford University Press, 2007.

Willis, Jim. *100 Media Moments That Changed America*. Santa Barbara: Greenwood, 2009.

Wineburg, Sam, and others. "Evaluating Information: The Cornerstone of Civic Online Reasoning." Stanford Digital Repository, 2016. purl.stanford.edu/fv751yt5934.

Winn, Conchita Hassell. "Spanish-Language Newspapers." In Handbook of Texas Online. Texas State Historical Association. tshaonline.org/handbook/online/ articles/ees18.

INDEX

153

INDEX

INDEX

Photo Credits

All rights reserved; 77 (LO), Nick Ut/AP/Shutterstock; 78 (hand), M-vector/Shutterstock; 78 (UP), Gift of Philip van Ingen, 1942/Metropolitan Museum of Art; 78 (LO RT), The Picture Art Collection/Alamy Stock Photo; 78 (LO LE), Everett Historical/Shutterstock; 79 (UP), DOONESBURY © 2019 G. B. Trudeau. Reprinted with permission of Andrews Mcmeel Syndication. All rights reserved.; 79 (LO RT), Atta Kenare/AFP via Getty Images; 79 (LO LE), Barbara Smaller/The New Yorker Collection/The Cartoon Bank; 80 (UP), AsexuaL/Shutterstock; 80 (LO), Chronicle/Alamy Stock Photo; 81 (UP), NASA/JSC; 82 (ALL), Library of Congress Prints and Photographs Division; 83 (UP LE), Library of Congress Prints and Photographs Division; 83 (CTR RT), Yonhap News/YNA/Newscom; 83 (LO RT), LeonP/Shutterstock; 83 (tree), Library of Congress Prints and Photographs Division; 83 (horse), Library of Congress Prints and Photographs Division; 83 (scene), Library of Congress Prints and Photographs Division; 85, Bettmann/Getty Images

CHAPTER 4

86, VadimGuzhva/Adobe Stock; 87, sebra/Adobe Stock; 88, Chameleons Eye/Shutterstock; 89 (UP), nikodash/Adobe Stock; 89 (CTR), Christophe Simon/AFP via Getty Images; 89 (LO), Prostock-studio/Adobe Stock; 89 (INSET), Tierney/Adobe Stock; 90, Joe Raedle/Staff/Getty Images; 91, khudoliy/Adobe Stock; 92, Schwarz/AP Photo; 93, CNN/Everett Collection, Inc.; 94, Nicole Glass Photography/Shutterstock; 95 (UP), jeff Metzger/Adobe Stock; 95 (LO), Lawrence Jackson/AP Photo; 96 (UP), Reuters/Charles Platiau; 96 (CTR), Jay L. Clendenin/Los Angeles Times via Getty Images; 97, Maurice Savage/Alamy Stock Photo; 98, zendograph/Adobe Stock; 99, Brendan Smialowski/Getty Images for Meet the Press; 100, Stephen J. Boitano/NBCU Photo Bank/NBC Universal via Getty Images; 101 (UP), Storms Media Group/Alamy Live News; 101 (CTR), Astrid Stawiarz/MSNBC/NBCU Photo Bank/NBC Universal via Getty Images; 101 (LO), fotofabrika/Adobe Stock; 102 (hand), Neyro/Adobe Stock; 102, Dominik Bindl/Getty Images; 103 (UP), Martin Harvey/Getty Images; 103 (LO), Reuters/Eduardo Munoz; 104 (UP), Gil C/Shutterstock; 104 (pen), J. background/Shutterstock; 104 (paper), Photo_SS/Shutterstock; 105 (UP), Virginia Sherwood/Walt Disney Television via Getty Images; 105 (LO), Cindy Ord/Getty Images for TIME 100 Health Summit; 107, Planetpix/Alamy Stock Photo; 107 (INSETS), AP Photo; 108 (phone), guteksk7/Shutterstock; 109 (hand), Neyro/Adobe Stock; 109, Photo 12/Alamy Stock Photo; 110 (hand), M-vector/Shutterstock; 110 (UP RT), Kaspars Grinvalds/Adobe Stock; 110 (LO), Steve Liss/The LIFE Images Collection via Getty Images/Getty Images; 111, sdecoret/Adobe Stock; 113, John Stanmeyer/National Geographic Image Collection

CHAPTER 5

114, Facundo Arrizabalaga/EPA/Shutterstock; 115, Vitaly Korovin/Shutterstock; 116 (UP), PNPImages/Shutterstock; 116 (LO), pabrady63/Adobe Stock; 117 (UP), Charles Platiau/Reuters; 117 (LO), Antonio Gravante/Adobe Stock; 118 (UP), Africa Studio/Shutterstock; 118 (CTR), Fulton History; 118 (LO), Eric Isselee/Shutterstock; 119 (hand), M-vector/Shutterstock; 119 (LO RT), Jae C. Hong/AP Photo; 119 (LO), ChaiwutNNN/Adobe Stock; 120, Dmytro Smaglov/Adobe Stock; 121 (UP), khosrork/Adobe Stock; 121 (LO), Hurst Photo/Shutterstock; 122, Pixel Homunculus Stock/Shutterstock; 123 (UP), Vitaly Korovin/Shutterstock; 123 (LO), 3D generator/Adobe Stock; 124, georgejmclittle/Adobe Stock; 125 (UP LE), turbaliska/Shutterstock; 125 (UP RT), AP Images/zz/Dennis Van Tine/STAR MAX/IPx; 125 (LO), peshkova/Adobe Stock; 126 (UP), BSPollard/Getty Images; 126 (LO), pixelrobot/Adobe Stock; 127 (UP), Lyudmyla Kharlamova/Shutterstock; 127 (LO), pondus369/

Shutterstock; 128 (A), MediaProduction/iStockphoto; 128 (B), Angelov/Adobe Stock; 128 (C), imageBROKER/Alamy Stock Photo; 129 (D), Design Pics Inc/Alamy Stock Photo; 129 (E), Katherine Feng/Minden Pictures; 129 (F), Lissandra Melo/Shutterstock; 130, Verastuchelova/Dreamstime; 131 (UP), PhotoPlus+/Adobe Stock; 131 (LO), Smit/Shutterstock; 133, published with permission of Nirmal Purja, Copyright 2019

CHAPTER 6

134-135, metamorworks/Adobe Stock; 135, Talaj/Adobe Stock; 136-137 (BACKGROUND), TWStock/Shutterstock; 136, Tatiana Shepeleva/Adobe Stock; 137 (UP), motttive/Shutterstock; 137 (LO), cherezoff/Adobe Stock; 139 (UP), dragonstock/Adobe Stock; 139 (LO), charnsitr/Shutterstock; 140, Syda Productions/Adobe Stock; 141, metamorworks/Adobe Stock

END MATTER

142 (RT), Sensay/Adobe Stock; 142 (LE), vladischern/Adobe Stock; 143, Kaspars Grinvalds/Adobe Stock; 144 (UP), Courtesy Naftali Bendavid; 144 (LO), Courtesy Marcia Bullard; 145 (UP LE), Courtesy Lydia L Chávez; 145 (CTR RT), Courtesy Michael Cottman; 145 (CTR LE), Mark Thiessen/National Geographic Image Collection; 145 (LO RT), Courtesy Clark Hoyt; 146 (UP RT), Courtesy Anna Kassinger; 146 (CTR RT), BrAt82/Adobe Stock; 146 (CTR LE), Courtesy Linda Kauss; 146 (LO RT), Courtesy Brent Kendall; 147 (UP), Courtesy of the Washington Post; 147 (CTR), Courtesy Trevy McDonald; 147 (LO), Courtesy Robin Sproul; 148, vchalup/Adobe Stock; 149 (UP), Kozini/Shutterstock; 151, Artur Widak/NurPhoto via Getty Images; 153, Hurst Photo/Shutterstock; 155, charles taylor/Shutterstock; 157, Dja65/Shutterstock; 159, 3D generator/Adobe Stock; 160, sdecoret/Adobe Stock

For more information, visit nationalgeographic.com, call 1-877-873-6846, or write to the following address:

National Geographic Partners
1145 17th Street N.W.
Washington, DC 20036-4688 U.S.A.

Visit us online at nationalgeographic.com/books.

For librarians and teachers: nationalgeographic.com/books/librarians-and-educators

More for kids from National Geographic: natgeokids.com

National Geographic Kids magazine inspires children to explore their world with fun yet educational articles on animals, science, nature, and more. Using fresh storytelling and amazing photography, *Nat Geo Kids* shows kids ages 6 to 14 the fascinating truth about the world—and why they should care. kids.nationalgeographic.com/subscribe

For rights or permissions inquiries, please contact National Geographic Books Subsidiary Rights: bookrights@natgeo.com

Designed by Rachael Hamm Plett, Moduza Design; Callie Broaddus; and Eva Absher-Schantz.

ACKNOWLEDGMENTS

I am humbled by the many accomplished and talented people who contributed their time and expertise to this project. First, I want to thank Susan Goldberg, editor in chief of *National Geographic* magazine, for her insightful foreword and her support of this important book. I am also indebted to the brain trust of esteemed journalists and media experts who took the time to review this book so carefully. My deepest thanks go to Teresa Palomo Acosta, Naftali Bendavid, Marcia Bullard, Lydia Chávez, Michael H. Cottman, Clark Hoyt, Anna Kassinger, Linda Kauss, Brent Kendall, Ann E. Marimow, Trevy A. McDonald, and Robin Sproul. This work has benefited tremendously from their years of experience as well as their thoughtful, honest, and perceptive comments. I also want to thank the amazing team at National Geographic Kids for entrusting me with this project, which is so necessary at this moment in history. Thank you to my incredible editors, Erica Green, Kate Hale, and Shelby Lees, for their patience, intelligence, encouragement, and vision; to Rachel Buchholz, for thinking of me for this project; to designers Rachael Hamm Plett, Callie Broaddus, and Eva Absher-Schantz and photo editors Lori Epstein and Sarah J. Mock, for making the layouts sing; to intrepid researcher Michelle Harris, for keeping us true to the facts and mission of this book; and to production editors Joan Gossett and Molly Reid, for dotting every *i* and crossing every *t*. Most of all, I want to thank my husband, Bill, for his love and patience as I wrote into the wee hours of the morning and for his unwavering support all along the way. —Robin Terry Brown

Library of Congress Cataloging-in-Publication Data

Names: Brown, Robin Terry, author.
Title: Breaking the news / Robin Terry Brown.
Description: Washington : National Geographic Kids, 2020. | Includes bibliographical references and index. | Audience: Ages 10 and up | Audience: Grades 7-9
Identifiers: LCCN 2019036140 | ISBN 9781426338885 (hardcover) | ISBN 9781426338892 (library binding)
Subjects: LCSH: Journalism--History. | Fake news--Juvenile literature.
Classification: LCC PN4731 .B78 2020 | DDC 070.9--dc23
LC record available at https://lccn.loc.gov/2019036140

Printed in Hong Kong
20/PPHK/1